Vampires

A Bloodthirsty History in Art and Literature

Diana Phillips-Summers

Astrolog Publishing House

Cover Design: Na'ama Yaffe
Language Consultant: Marion Duman
Layout and Graphics: Daniel Akerman
Illustrations: H. Kano
Production Manager: Dan Gold

P.O. Box 1123, Hod Hasharon 45111, Israel
Tel: 972-9-7412044
Fax: 972-97442714

Published by Astrolog Publishing House 2004

Highlights from the contents

First European testimonies

When Austria seized control of the lands on the eastern borders of Europe, a new phenomenon came to the notice of the conquerors: the local population had espoused a custom of exhuming the dead in order to "kill" them again. The researchers who witnessed these ceremonies documented and reported what they had seen, and these testimonies spread and reached Austria, Germany, France and England. The other European countries were also nourished by these rumors, and soon the strange events in Transylvania became one of the folkloristic milestones in the history of Western culture. The Slavic vampire, known by the name of Vapir or Upir, resembled other European creatures that bore different names and appearances, in accordance with the culture from which they had sprung. The fact that the phenomenon did not characterize only godforsaken and primitive villages but rather was found in many other places as well turned the vampire into a myth that steadily gained strength until it became what we know today.

One of the reasons why so many people continued investigating and interpreting the phenomenon was the attempt to understand it. The acknowledgment of its existence is halfway to solving it. As early as the Middle Ages, and also later, European scholars were astonished to discover

vampires stories in distant cultures such as China, Indonesia and the Philippines. It seemed that vampires lived everywhere, and what they all had in common was the fact that they were dead people who had, in most cases, passed away in an untimely manner. They refused to remain in the next world and insisted on returning to this world in order to kill their living neighbors and friends.

The belief in the existence of vampires stems from the ancient belief that death causes death. This may be difficult for the modern person to comprehend, since over the generations he has lost the link he used to have with his profound intuition, that inner place in which there are reservoirs of comprehension that have nothing to do with pure logic. Out of this unknown, the primeval vampire was born, followed by the modern vampire, too. Human intuition, accompanied by all of those clues and testimonies, did not provide the researchers with a single accurate and certain piece of knowledge or rational reason for the existence of vampires. They possessed nothing but doubts. Despite those doubts, the mysterious vampire persisted in its refusal to die.

The image of a vampire

The question of whether it is a person – a man or a woman – or some other monstrously evil creature that appears in the form of the human body is the key to the popular understanding of the belief in the existence of vampires both in the past and today. Even if the shape of the vampire is human, it has various grotesque versions, and overall it represents a creature with an image that is a combination of the living human body and decaying death. Vampires are most repulsive from the visual point of view: long, curling fingernails; pallid skin, except for the moments following bloodsucking; their eyes look dead, but they have a hypnotic gaze; their teeth are long and primed to attack. Vampires engender a great deal of psychological revulsion as well: they are malicious and immoral; they exist outside the bounds of normal society – and are therefore threatening; because they are bloodthirsty, they kill mercilessly; and they have the ability to turn their unwilling victims into vampires like themselves.

The man or woman who becomes a vampire is condemned to an eternal life of torment. From now on, they will live on the other side of life, in a cold, dark and isolated world, instead of resting peacefully in the next world and waiting quietly for their soul's turn to be reincarnated in a new body and return to life fully.

Vampires are afraid of sunlight, and for this reason they wander around gloomy forests, isolated villages, mountains and abandoned castles. In the modern world, they also live on dark streets and corners in the center of the world's big cities. Moreover, they are afraid of Christian icons, wolfsbane and especially garlic. They are deterred by water in which they cannot walk, habitually sleep in coffins, and prefer the blood of young virgins to that of middle-age men, even though when push comes to shove, the blood of any live human being is welcome. They are generally accompanied by an evil servant who does the "dirty work" during the day, and they tend to carry the earth from their graves with them wherever they go.

Other perhaps less well-known facts about vampires are as follows: Vampires behave very circumspectly with regard to their weaknesses and fears; there are female vampires just as there are male vampires; there are visible vampires as well as vampires that can change shape at will; and there are vampires that choose to take things that are valuable to their victims from them – such as their youth, their hope or their love – rather than suck their blood.

The image of the aristocratic vampire – of which broad dramatic use was made in literature, theater and particularly film during the 20th century – was generally identical in description: a tall thin man, dressed in a black suit and a long black cloak. At first sight, he resembles an unmistakably elegant figure, but another glance reveals his smile with the long fangs, his foul breath, his pallid skin and his nails that are as long as an animal's claws.

Having said that, the popular folkloristic vampire was different than the literary vampire that was first created in John Polidori's story, "*The Vampire*" (which was based on Lord Byron's original idea). According to the stories and testimonies that were collected from the inhabitants of Eastern Europe in the Middle Ages, the vampire is not a person who looks pale, but rather one with healthy coloring, apparently because of his bloodsucking habits. Nineteenth-century studies turned the mythology into a manifesto, and there are as many different variations of the appearance of the folkloristic vampire as there are European countries of origin. What they all have in common is the assumption that the vampire's hair grows in a strange way: his eyebrows are thick and joined and his hands are very hairy. Most Romanian vampires had short tails covered with hair. The prevailing belief at the time that vampires were also responsible for spreading various diseases and epidemics originated in the marks of blood that could be seen on their faces, and from the fact that death occurred around them with suspicious suddenness. The only thing the literary vampire and the ancient popular vampire had in common was their long white teeth, which had a single purpose: drawing out and sucking the victims' blood.

In the villages of Eastern Europe, just like in 20th-century movies, vampires lay quietly in their graves as if tranquilly awaiting their fate. In this state of trance, they were less dangerous and more vulnerable. This state reflects their non-human nature, and, more than any of the physical signs that have been mentioned up till now, it may actually be these non-human properties that are more dangerous, since they are not immediately evident. These properties include the hypnotic gaze of the vampire; to his great ability to maneuver people by means of emotional and psychological manipulations; the fact that the problems of the world and human existence are meaningless to him and he is totally indifferent to them; and his strong desire to imitate life. It is therefore advisable to stay away from anyone who displays such properties, for he may be a vampire who is waiting for us to fall into a trap that will lead to certain death.

The creation of a vampire

From the various testimonies, we learn that these are creatures that were nothing more than completely ordinary human beings prior to undergoing a change. The vampire's body is a corpse that mysteriously continues to operate and function for generations, until the moment it "dies" for the second time – this time as a vampire. We also know that vampires' victims become vampires themselves, and that the vampire existence is as infectious as an epidemic.

However, that is not the whole story. There are still unanswered questions. For instance, are only certain people chosen to become vampires, or is any one of us liable to discover that he is a vampire one day? Does any human blood satisfy the vampire, or only the blood of certain people? The fact that vampires always operated clandestinely did not permit these questions to be answered. Thus we will never know if the inhabitants of the villages of Transylvania – who were the first to testify to the existence of vampires – were frightened by the soul of the dead person or by the corpse that rose from its grave in the night and returned to it before daybreak. Since the witnesses are all dead today, only circumstantial evidence remains.

In her book, *Interview with the Vampire*, Anne Rice provides the first detailed description of how a vampire is born. Rice basically answers the question of what happens in the dead person's body while he is turning into a vampire. She adopts new physical laws that go beyond the ordinary human existence with which we are familiar, thereby making life outside of time and the existence of vampires possible.

In Rice's book, the vampire Louis tells a young journalist how he became a vampire in 1791, when he was only 25. Louis remained alive after a terrible tragedy in his family, but felt heavily responsible for the disaster that had occurred. His life became fraught with guilt feelings and a lack of faith. Lestat the vampire pounced on Louis and drank almost all of his blood. Louis became debilitated and almost lifeless. A few nights later, Lestat returned to him, and in the darkness, the weak

Louis thought that it was the doctor who had come to call on him. When Lestat moved near to the light of the oil lamp, Louis saw that this was no ordinary human being: His eyes were gray and his hands white and long… I saw him and the special aura around him... I had never met such a creature before. I forgot myself entirely... The moment the creature spoke to me and told me what I was about to become, my past disappeared.

The first step, therefore, in becoming a vampire is hypnosis. The vampire hypnotizes his victim, promising him eternal life outside of human life, values and commitment. The longing to repress and forget, to give oneself over to a life devoid of obligation as well as pleasure – this is the door through which the vampire invites his victim to pass. He transforms him into a supernatural creature that possesses an existence that parallels human life but is also completely separate from it, since he must also be nourished by it. The yearning for eternal life includes superhuman power, and it is in fact the greatest sin of the ego. Turning into a vampire is the punishment for this sin.

I perceived the process of my transformation into a vampire in two ways: on the one hand, I was enchanted, he simply invited me to the bed of death, and on the other, I had a desire for self-destruction, and now not only could I destroy myself, but someone else as well, says Louis. Except that at this stage, he still has human emotions and he still wants to die, since he finds his existence as a vampire intolerable and he does not want it. Then Lestat the vampire moves to the next stage: the physical attack. This stage will conclude the process of Louis' transformation from a person into a vampire.

Louis relates that he remembers that Lestat's lips drank his blood and caused the hairs on his body to stand on end. His body was completely quiet while Lestat sucked the blood from him. To complete the ceremony, Lestat bit his own wrist and offered it to Louis so that he could also drink the blood and thereby understand for the first time what pleasure was entailed in his life as a vampire.

Then Louis hears a loud noise that initially sounds to him like a roar and then like the beating of a large drum. The noise increases until it fills his body and all of his senses. More beating is heard, and Lestat releases his hand from Louis' bite. Louis understands that the sound of drumbeats he heard was nothing more than the sound of his own and Lestat's powerfully beating hearts. Each one penetrated the other's heart at the moment of sucking. At the end of this experience, Louis actually crosses the border between the human world and the supernatural world. Now he begins to see the world around him with eyes filled with mystery, with the eyes of a vampire... I saw colors and shapes as if I were seeing them for the first time. Lestat began to laugh, and his laugh sounded metallic and fitted into the wildness of the loud sound of his heartbeat... It took me time until I learned to separate the two sounds.

This incident is actually the first attempt in literature to describe in detail the way a vampire sees, hears and feels after the transformation he has undergone. Since he is already dead, the vampire is already entrenched outside of the framework of time that dominates our human actions, thoughts and emotions. Now he feels, hears and senses everything while at a distance from time, and in this way he can also see reality fully, beyond the limits of time. His senses have become honed. It sounds logical, since now he is more "bestial" than he was as an ordinary person. As an animal, he is condemned to kill

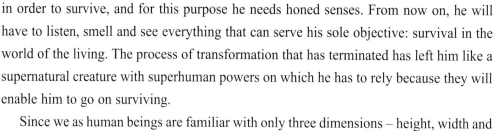

in order to survive, and for this purpose he needs honed senses. From now on, he will have to listen, smell and see everything that can serve his sole objective: survival in the world of the living. The process of transformation that has terminated has left him like a supernatural creature with superhuman powers on which he has to rely because they will enable him to go on surviving.

Since we as human beings are familiar with only three dimensions – height, width and depth – it is difficult for us to understand the way in which the "non-dead" perceive the world around them. We do not have any experience outside of the three-dimensional framework, and for this reason it is difficult for us to understand the phenomenon. Vampires live in the world of shadows, a world in which things have neither existence nor importance, a world in which time does not exist, life is eternal, and the various powers control everything and move in directions that are difficult for us to understand.

Louis describes the end of the process of his transformation into a vampire in these words: I felt that I was dead as a person, and at the same time completely alive as a vampire.

In her book, Rice also states that: the victim who becomes a vampire never bleeds to death. He is nourished with a great deal of attention, helps in the development of the senses of the vampire, learns how to kill, to look for coffins, to wander through the world without arousing suspicion, to live a life of luxury as a lord or a lady. The transformation process can be described in human terms as 'falling in love.'

...To be, or not to be: that is the question:
Whether 'tis nobler in the mind to suffer
The slings and arrows of outrageous fortune,
Or to take arms against a sea of troubles,
And by opposing end them? To die: to sleep:
No more; and by a sleep to say we end...

The revenant (living dead)

*I*t is important to distinguish between those who have experienced the transformation process from a person into a vampire and the victims who do not necessarily become vampires. The revenant is a person who was attacked by a vampire, died and was buried, and afterwards rose up from his grave. The revenant is no longer alive, and although blood has been sucked out of him to the point of death, he has not turned into a vampire. The death of the revenant is liable to be caused by the shock engendered by the encounter with the vampire or the loss of blood. His spirit, too, continues to roam through the nights in search of victims. He kills anyone anywhere, quite openly. His appearance differs from that of the vampire: He is not meticulous in the way he dresses, since he has no intention of making his body indestructible after death. The revenant chooses to present a far more repulsive and monstrous exterior than that of the vampire.

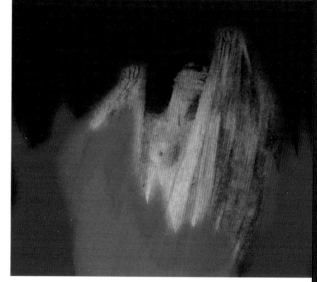

The life of the revenant is very different than the vampire's life. The revenant experiences many more difficulties because of his lack of sophistication, as opposed to the vampire, who has learned how to live in comfort and luxury. What they have in common is the attack, which is generally carried out by biting and sucking blood from the neck or the heart region. The revenant's victims become revenants themselves, whether these are human beings or animals. This phenomenon was known as "the plague of vampires" in the villages of Transylvania, and there it could reach a point in which the entire village became a community of such revenants.

The nature of death

When the oxygen runs out, the blood becomes dark, and we expect the body to change color. However, because of gravity, the blood continues flowing naturally toward the lower part of the body, and for this reason, the face appears to be paler than the other parts of the body.

A phenomenon that has been reported more than once is that of corpses that suddenly "dried out" during burial. Of course, it is easy to contradict this by claiming that it is a question of preconceptions as a result of the fear of vampires. However, if we try to explain the phenomenon from the biological point of view, we will find that between the throat and the trachea, there are certain chemicals and fluids that continue to function after death. In fact, there is a post-mortem system that continues to operate. After the fluids in the body have dried up, the muscles and tissues in the abdomen produce a counter-reaction that causes the corpse to become erect in a sitting position. If the arms are resting diagonally on the thighs, in a position in which it is generally customary to lay out the dead, they may suddenly lift forward in a manner that resembles a real horror movie. In general, the corpse remains

in the position it was in at the moment of death. If a stick were introduced into the hands of such a corpse, it would not be unusual if the dead person's hand continued to grasp it without letting it go. The preservation of a corpse depends on several factors: micro-organisms, air, humidity, temperature and the presence of bacteria. The body can be preserved in several ways when it is buried in the earth, especially if the earth is organic, natural and warm. In such a case, the tissues can be preserved.

The numerous phenomena of revenants that were reported in the villages of Eastern Europe over 400 years ago can be explained by means of the above biological theories. When the graves were opened, it was found that in some of the corpses, the outer skin had disappeared, and beneath it, new fresh skin had grown. This could refer to the epidermal layer that fell off, and in fact what appeared is not "new" skin, but rather a new layer that looks fresher and more colorful than the epidermal layer that covered the corpse when it was still alive. The sighs that were heard emitting from the dead when their graves were opened can be explained as the gases that accumulated in the dead body. The micro-organisms produced gas, mainly methane, penetrated the tissues, accumulated, and were expelled audibly via the trachea, since they did not have any

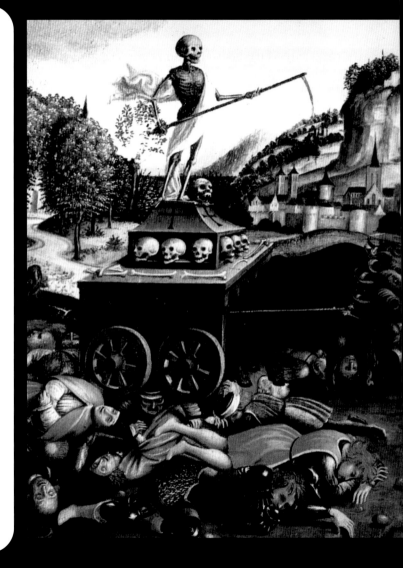

other pipe through which they could escape from the body. The bleeding from the nose and the mouth can also be explained medically as the body's post-mortem reaction. Blood may continue to be liquid after death, and this can also explain the fact that it gushes out after a stake has pierced the corpse's heart.

During the Dark Ages, a belief took root in the soil of isolated villages whose inhabitants were gripped by the fear of the unknown. According to this belief, if a person wanted to die, died a strange or violent death, or died under some other extraordinary circumstances, it was a sign that he had been punished for the sins he committed during his lifetime. The changes that took place in the body of such a person could confirm this fact, and as a result of the loss of his humanity, he would become a vampire. Thus, this fear, which, in the case of vampires became hysterical terror, turned into something that was inseparable from bad luck. Accordingly, suspicious behavior among the dead could indicate different things. Among the gypsies, for instance, if the corpse did not decompose shortly after burial, or alternatively, if its color changed, it was a sign that the dead person had turned into a vampire. In other cultures, too, it was found that there is no consistency regarding this topic. Sometimes the indication of the existence of a vampire depends on the change that takes place in the corpse, and sometimes exactly the opposite: in the total and threatening lack of change following death.

From this we can understand that from the physiological point of view, we cannot in fact differentiate unequivocally between an ordinary dead body and a vampire. The reinforcement for this or any other assumption can be found in the answer to the question: After the dead person was buried, did a rapid series of deaths occur in the environs? If so, somebody must have caused them.

Supernatural life

L et's try to understand how a vampire lives after the moment of death. To this end, we must leave the physical world of the dead and turn toward the supernatural, beyond the grave. One of the various theories that exist about the topic claims that vampires are not really dead, but rather in a "coma", unconscious, that is, like "vegetables". Only after they are discovered do they come back to life, and then they spread fear and killing around them. However, this theory is not convincing because we already know that vampires undergo a process of physical decomposition that leads to absolute death, and it does not seem as if vampires have been in a "coma" after spending years in their graves.

A more modern theory propounded by Karl Meuli states that "the quality of our thinking does not enable us to grasp our non-existence." Not just that, but we are unable to grasp the death of another person. If this is the case, we have to turn to some other place. As mentioned, many witnesses reported that it is not possible to catch the vampire or kill him while he is roaming around free, because he is nothing but a ghost, a wandering soul. Moreover, the only way to kill a vampire is when he is in his coffin, preferably in his grave, at the moment when his soul is resting in its place of residence.

The fact that vampires were seen when they were talking to themselves reinforces the belief that they have two souls, each of which is dedicated to the elimination of humanity. One soul is evil, and it can take over a living body and turn it into a vampire. The other leaves the body and returns to it in order to revive it once more. So long as more victims whose blood can nourish the dead body can be found, it will continue to exist. The other soul, the one that does not find peace after physical death, repeatedly tries to return to live in the human body and control the soul that resides in it. This is an evil soul, whose role on earth has not yet ended; it is seeking revenge. It is therefore obvious that the soul is linked to the body from which it emerges, even though it is completely separate from it.

The soul of the vampire resides in the heart – and this is the reason why a wooden stake must be driven through the vampire's heart in order to achieve its absolute death. Subsequently, it is advisable to burn the body and sprinkle the ashes

in water. Another widespread belief in the supernatural world states that the soul is unable to choose the body in which it will reside, and sometimes it assumes different forms: it becomes invisible, formless and white, or it adopts the shape of the body in which it resided prior to death. A soul can appear as a breath, a shadow, light or a candle, a white dove, or even a bee. A soul that previously belonged to a particularly evil person can also appear in the form of a small black heart.

In other ancient primitive cultures, too, it was believed that the soul was linked to its body and for that reason could leave it only at the moment of death or during sleep. That was one of the explanations for the changes that take place in the body during sleep as opposed to wakefulness. This is why children were taught for generations to pray before going to sleep that their souls would not be taken from them while they were asleep.

Great fear exists with regard to the possibility that the soul will remain trapped outside of the body and will not be able to return to it. A broken mirror is bad luck. This superstition originates from the notion that a mirror contains the reflection of the soul. This is why it is believed that after a person's death, the mirrors in the house must be covered so that the dead person's soul is not reflected in the mirror and will not return to reside in the corpse. It must be remembered that the image of the vampire is never reflected in a mirror. In certain parts of Europe, it was customary to empty out vessels filled with water in

which reflections could also appear, just like in a mirror. In Romania, it was customary to cover all such vessels at night for fear that the spirit would fall into one of them and drown during its nocturnal wanderings. In Macedonia, the exact opposite was customary: They would leave the vessels and the containers full of water beside the grave so that if the evil spirit was inside it, it would fall into the water and would not go out to roam around and bother others. According to another custom, water was poured between the place of death and the dead person's burial place in order to create a barrier between the dead and the living, thus preventing the spirit from coming back to life. These beliefs prevailed in Europe prior to the Industrial Revolution, when there were not many mirrors around, and the ones that existed were of such poor quality that it was hardly possible to identify the images reflected in them…

People also believed in the ability of the eyes to reflect images and to trap the souls of lost children. This is the reason why contact with the gaze of the dead person and with what is liable to be reflected in his eyes must be avoided. It must be remembered that vampires are in the habit of trapping their victims with their eyes by hypnotizing them and staring them to death sometimes. In many places in the world, this belief led to

the widespread action of closing the person's eyes at the moment of death, even though the modern explanation for this is to allow the dead to rest in peace.

Many people believed that the next world is nothing but a mirror of this world in which everything is the opposite, and the souls in it seek to return to this world via the bodies of the dead in order to continue living in it. In order to ensure that the spirit leaves the dead person never to return, it is customary in certain places to open the doors and windows of the house and clean every corner following the moment of death, in case the lost soul is hiding in one of them. The length of the mourning period is also parallel to the length of time it takes for the corpse to avoid any danger of the soul returning to reside in it. In Spain and southern Italy, women are in the habit of mourning their fathers and husbands for ten years, and their brothers and sons for five years. During the period of mourning, they refrain from using makeup, cut their hair and wear black clothes – all in order to be identified as mourners, so that if the dead person decides to come back to life, he will know whom to approach…

Who has the "privilege" of becoming a vampire?

Everyone is liable to become a vampire after death, but some are more destined to do so than others. The latter include people who were excommunicated from the community during their lifetime or committed suicide, faithless people, victims of violent deaths, women who were suspected of being witches, werewolves, whores and highwaymen, and any other person who was not properly baptized or who was not buried in a proper Christian ceremony and whose burial was not completed. There are unlucky people who become vampires through no fault of their own. These include infants who were born with teeth, with very dark or excessively blue eyes, with marks

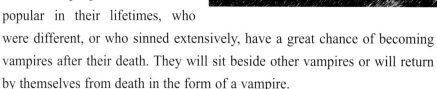

on their bodies, with an extra nipple, with one nostril, with a cleft palate, with a protruding tail-like spine, and with excessive hair. All of the people who were not popular in their lifetimes, who

were different, or who sinned extensively, have a great chance of becoming vampires after their death. They will sit beside other vampires or will return by themselves from death in the form of a vampire.

The life of the modern vampire

After he has been created, the vampire lives in poverty for several years, during which learns about his abilities. The next stage in his life is to obtain a castle in a distant and uninhabited region, or a large house that meets his needs, in order to have room for hiding coffins and his victims. The modern vampire refrains from rubbing elbows with the local population and tries not to be too conspicuous in order not to arouse suspicion. His relations with his neighbors are parasitic, that is, he will use them for his pleasures and for his survival and will endow them with his material capabilities. He does not want them to suspect him, but without a doubt he shrouds himself in mystery and engenders a great deal of doubt in the public – sometimes as a deliberate policy – in order to nurture the secret fear of him in the people around him.

The life of the modern vampire is rather ascetic. For the sake of the air of mystery, he finds himself living on the edge of society, keeping a low profile, and maintaining contact only with those who give him pleasure. In general, he is a great intellectual, since he has accumulated a great deal of knowledge during his life, which has gone on for generations and hundreds of years, and he knows how to impress other people with his knowledge of culture, literature, art and music. Having said that, there are a few problems he has to cope with in his desire to appear like everyone else. He does not eat at all and he does not live among people in daylight. He has to conceal the coffins he sleeps in very well, because when he is inside them, he is in a particularly vulnerable position. The coffin must be covered with good-quality silk with a layer of earth from the grave from which he rose.

The vampire's servant – a highly inspired figure in his own right – is generally a revenant that the vampire keeps for himself in a state of balance between life and death. The vampire can annihilate his servant totally at any time, and this is how he keeps him with him. The servant behaves as if he is hypnotized, and his job is to keep curious people such as students, doctors and researchers away from the place. Furthermore, he has to provide the vampire with his requisite nourishment, which includes mice and other small animals on which he has to live in the meantime. The vampire's servant is the person who is closest to his master, and he is the only one who knows the whole truth about his life. Without him, the vampire would be completely isolated. Two vampires can never live together because the need of both of them to kill in order to exist would exhaust the available supplies in the vicinity. The fact that both of them lust for human life would place them in a state of incessant conflict and would not enable them to lead a joint life.

The modern vampire lives like a lord and has to dress accordingly. He wears a long black cloak, which, when open, looks like bat's wings. It is made of smooth, shiny satin, and its size enables the vampire to hide inside it by hiding his head in his hands and becoming invisible, until he disappears completely.

Beneath the cloak, the vampire wears an elegant black tuxedo with tails that reach below his knees. His trousers are also black, his shirt white, and his collar stiffer and higher than normal in order to camouflage the deathly pallor of his face as much as possible. His neatly polished leather shoes complete his hypnotic presence.

The vampire never shows himself in full light and chooses to appear in rooms that are illuminated by the weak light of a candle. His movements are so fast that the human eye sometimes cannot discern them. That is because he lives beyond the boundaries of human time as we know it. In this 21th-century costume, the modern vampire can disguise himself after long years of study, and permit himself to continue becoming addicted to his pleasures with as few disturbances from the outside world as possible.

How to discover the existence of a vampire

People who have the feel and talent for discovering vampires were called "vampire catchers" and were given the name "Vampiritch" in Eastern European countries. In order to locate them, they would send a pure virgin on a white or black horse to the cemetery, and there, next to the vampire's grave, the horse would neigh and point out the place. An additional clue to the existence of vampires is the presence of small holes in the earth around the grave, through which, it was supposed, the vampire would leave his grave on foggy nights.

How to exorcise a vampire

*T*he belief stated that there was no remedy that was completely effective against the existence of vampires. Having said that, it was known that holy water – which symbolizes the source of life – as well as symbols that are linked to the Christian cross, were capable of deflecting the vampire and debilitating him. Another of his weaknesses was the necessity to return to his grave at dawn, before cock-crow. However, the final elimination of the vampire was only possible by driving a wooden stake through his heart.

If vampires are born nonetheless, there are several ways to prevent their attack. The most widespread of these is the use of garlic. The powerful odor of the garlic deters the vampire and chases him away, so it is customary to place cloves of garlic in the dead person's grave and hang a chain of garlic around the necks of the members of his family, in the rooms of the house – especially around doors and windows, at the heads of beds and even in the farmyard. Another herb that proved itself to be no less effective is the poisonous wolfsbane, which is used in the same way as garlic.

Throughout the years, it has been proved that the use of garlic is effective against diseases and epidemics, and it serves as an excellent natural "antibiotic". Just as garlic can repel plagues and other diseases, so it is effective against "a plague of vampires", which also has an unpleasant odor and an unknown origin, just like other plagues.

There are other ways to avoid vampires, the most primitive of which is placing an object of some kind in the dead person's grave, something that will satisfy the corpse's needs and prevent it from returning to life. In this way, all the evil that threatens to disturb its peaceful rest in its grave is removed. In ancient Greece, it was customary to place coins on dead people's faces. In many cultures, food was placed in the coffins in the belief that the next world was similar to this world, and there too the dead have to eat, just like they did when they were alive. The food was solid or liquid and placed in jars and dishes.

And if the dead need food, the ancient mind presumed that they also needed to occupy themselves with manual labor. In many farming villages, it was customary to bury the dead person with a scythe – the archetypal symbol of the harvest – at his side. This, apparently, is the source of the depiction of death as a skeleton carrying a scythe, a figure that cuts life down. The assumption was that food and manual labor would keep the corpse and its soul busy, thereby relinquishing its desire to return to the world of the living.

In order to prevent the vampire's soul from uniting with its body, it was customary to place a particular object in the corpse's mouth. In Romania, garlic was favored, in Greece, a piece of bread, and in Saxony, a lemon. In other places, the dead were buried with their mouths facing downward, so that they could not see their

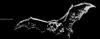

way out of the grave. Because of its narcotic effect, poppyseed was sprinkled outside the grave so as to encourage the dead person to sleep rather than roam through the land of the living. In Russia, it was customary to sprinkle poppyseed inside the coffin so that the dead person would busy himself counting them.

According to another custom, a thorn was inserted beneath the dead person's tongue, so that if he turned into  a vampire, he would be pricked while sucking his victim's blood. In Romania, sharpened stakes were driven into the graves so as to prevent the corpse from rising up out of its grave. If it did so, it would be pierced and would die again. Many skeletons were found in their graves with their knees and/or their elbows tied together. In Bulgaria, corpses were found that were buried rolled up in carpets. These methods employed force in order to compel the body not to get up from its desired prone position. However, the ropes were tied very loosely because of the belief that knots inside a grave would jeopardize the dead person's ability to move on to his next incarnation.

In Wallachia in Romania, weeping for the dead was prohibited. Instead, the friends and family would dance and sing and sometimes even lift up the corpse and dance with it, so that the evil spirits would think that they had come upon a festival and not a funeral, and that it was still a living body. In contrast, in Spain, Greece, southern Italy and other Catholic countries, it was customary to weep and mourn the dead. To this end, professional mourners were hired to lament the dead loudly during the funeral. The reason for this was that it was necessary to make the dead person's spirit believe that it was loved and would be duly missed. This would induce it to rest in peace in its grave rather than come back to life.

In Western Europe, ancient Egypt and Latin America, death was considered to be a transition from one state – life – to another – death. In these places, the burial was performed immediately after the death, and later on, the rites of a second burial were performed, during which the dead person's bones were covered, handled with great ceremony, and transferred to another burial place, where they were buried again for eternal rest. The reason for the second burial was to prevent the souls from finding their way back to life.

In many cultures, stones or rocks are placed on the body. The gravestones of today – even those that are decorated with angels – are an indication of this tradition. Another reason why gravestones were constructed vertically is, among other things, in order to prevent the dead from sitting up in their graves…

The assumption that the soul is still alive after burial was reinforced when shortly after burial, tiny lights were seen twinkling above the grave like fireflies in the dark. Today we know that these were not the souls burning after death or little fairies; there is a physiological explanation for the phenomenon: the decomposing body produces large quantities of methane gas, which becomes extremely flammable when mixed with oxygen. In the Middle Ages, when crevices and cracks were discovered in the earth covering the grave, people did not seek scientific explanations, but rather opted for the immediate assumption that the dead person was no doubt trying to get out of his grave. For that reason, there was an urgent need for another burial ceremony.

In many modern cemeteries today, it is customary to wait for a period of seven to twenty years and then open up the grave and exhume the dead person's bones. After burning them, the ashes are buried in another place. Ostensibly, the reason is to make room for other burials, but because of the tradition of a second burial, it would seem that this is not simply a matter of a practical solution. In Italy today, too, it is customary to exhume the bones of the dead in cemeteries after a certain period of time, place them in smaller coffins and bury them again.

Cremation is a well-known phenomenon in various cultures, especially in India. Cremating the body and releasing the soul precludes the possibility that the soul will return in the form of a revenant, but rather will continue reincarnating without disturbing other whole bodies. Indeed, throughout the history of these cultures, no plagues of vampires of any kind have been recorded. Nevertheless, cremating the body is a complicated process that requires a high temperature and patience, since it takes the body a long time to be completely consumed. This action was not feasible in the villages of Eastern Europe, and for that reason, the population there was compelled to make do with regular burial and run the risk of the return of the dead…

Since vampires became the province of the visual arts, especially movies, many movie directors have opted to use crucifixes and other Christian icons in order to keep vampires at bay. However, folklore and literature contain little evidence of this. Even though it was customary to paint crosses on the doors and windows of the houses in Serbia in order to protect the residents from vampire attacks, it would seem that other than this, neither God nor the church could do much against vampires. The people could only offer prayers to prevent the

return of the dead or perform religious ceremonies to increase the soul's chances of resting in peace.

As is well known, the classic method of killing a vampire is by driving a wooden stake into his heart, preferably when the vampire is lying in his coffin. In Russia, it was customary to use a stake that was made from the original cross, so they believed. In other countries, people preferred the wood from the original crown of thorns. In Dalmatia and Albania, the priests would drive special swords into the corpse before dawn.

After driving in the stake, it is advisable to drive it in further with the assistance of a sledgehammer. This is a dramatic action that was widely used by authors and moviemakers. Many movies feature the vampire lying in his coffin after the moment of death, dressed in his formal tuxedo, his dead eyes open and filled with hatred. After a blood-curdling scream, hundreds of years and generations pass over his pallid face all at once, until he turns into dust and ashes or into a mummy.

If there is no wooden stake at hand, a silver dagger will also help, even though it is usually used for getting rid of werewolves. After driving the stake or the dagger into the vampire's heart, it is customary to cut out the heart, burn it, and sprinkle the ashes into the flowing waters of a river. In Eastern Europe, there were people who would cut the head off the corpse and cover it with earth. They would burn the rest of the body and cast the ashes to the wind or bury them at a crossroads.

Medieval testimonies about the killing of vampires state that after death, the blood spurted upward into the air. The physiological reason for this is the accumulation of gases in the corpse. The post-mortem sigh – the classic vampire sigh – stems from the pressure that is exerted on the lungs and from the fact that the gases have no way of escaping other than through the trachea. Another explanation suggests the possibility that the vampire's wandering soul sighs deeply upon being released after being imprisoned for so many years. However, both of these explanations can be considered impossible just as they can be espoused as perfectly genuine…

It must be remembered that the vampire's existence repels and tortures him too, and for this reason, we would be doing him a service if we were to release his restless soul and kill him.

Who can kill a vampire?

*I*t is said that the killer must be highly motivated, since only people who seek revenge can withstand the terror and fear until the vampire is absolutely dead. In general, these are men whose fiancées were strangled or sucked to death by vampires, and now they are filled with vengeance. A vampire who does not die finally and completely because his murderer fled in fear in the middle of the act of killing him is far more dangerous than an ordinary vampire who is not threatened. Some people cover the "dead" vampire with shrouds or lengths of fabric before handling his corpse so that his blood will not "infect" the killer with a disease.

Sometimes it is the victim who musters enough courage to kill the vampire who keeps on sucking his blood and his life slowly and surely. If the victim overcomes the vampire, he has to stain the bites on his neck immediately with blood from the vampire's body, as if it were his own blood, and only by so doing will he be completely cured of the fateful vampire bites.

One of the first indications of the existence of the vampire myth was found in Persia (Iran of today) and Morocco as early as the prehistoric period: a jar featuring a drawing of a person wrestling with a monstrous creature that was trying to suck his blood.

There are people who claim that the legends about blood thirsty "revenants" originate in China of the sixth century BC. Other proof of the existence of the myth in ancient times was found in India, Malaysia and Polynesia, as well as among the Eskimos. According to the Aztecs, the blood of a young victim could ensure the fruitfulness of the earth.

*T*he origin of the vampire myth as we know it from the European culture can be found in ancient Greece – the cradle of Western civilization. The mysterious link between human blood and the world of the dead was presented for the first time in the eleventh book of Homer's *Odyssey*, which was written in the eighth or ninth century BC. There, the wandering hero, Odysseus, is described as sacrificing several sheep and collecting their blood, thereby calling on the spirits to help him on his journey. When they arrive, they drink the sheep's blood and by so doing, gain vitality and strength. The belief that blood has the power to intensify the strength and vitality of the human body continued until the Christian era.

*I*n ancient Egypt, it was found that worshipping the dead was characterized in ceremonies that featured a black bird, which the Egyptians believed to be none other than the flight of the soul at the moment of death and its journey to the world of shadows.

Empusai

Empusai was the daughter of the god Hecate, and resembled a demonic creature with a bronze leg. Empusai would turn into a young and beautiful woman in order to seduce men in their sleep. She is considered to be one of the most bloodthirsty gods of Greek mythology.

Lamiai

Lamiai was the daughter of the ancient king Belus. She was the lover of Zeus, and became the monster that devoured children or sucked their blood. Over the generations, her name became synonymous with a witch or a demonic creature.

Striges

Striges derived her name from the Latin word *strix*, a bird that drinks blood at night and is morphologically similar to the ancient sirens. According to the myth, Striges was a demonic woman with the body of a raven. She was in the habit of sucking the blood of infants and of drawing out the virility and vitality of sleeping men.

There is no direct link between the mythical figures mentioned above and the vampires we know today. The similarity lies in the terms *strige* and *strigoi*, which the Romans used since the seventh century in order to describe vampires. The difference is that in contrast to the modern vampires, Lamiai, Empusai and Striges are not revenants, but rather entities that can appear in the world of the living with the aim of seducing human beings. Later on, during the Christian era, the succubi would emerge from them. Succubi were demonic women who seduced young men in their sleep, had intercourse with them, and at the moment of climax drew their manhood out of them or killed them

The story of Lilith

One of the books of the Apocrypha (ancient Hebrew texts that are not included in the Old Testament) features the story of Lilith, who was in fact the first woman created, even before the creation of Eve. Lilith, who was disappointed by the sexual prowess of the first man, preferred to link up to the evil forces and become a demonic queen. The myth relates that she would drink the blood of infants, and just like in the Greek myth, she would draw the virility and vitality out of young men while they were sleeping.

Blood in Judaism

Because of the myth of Lilith, the Jewish Halacha prohibited the drinking of blood from live creatures. Jews have always had a complex relationship with blood. On the one hand, blood symbolized vitality and fertility and was sacred because of its ability to give the body life, just like God, who is the master of life and death. On the other, blood was always directly linked to the curse that Eve brought upon humanity after she fell victim to the temptation of evil.

According to the laws of Moses and Israel, menstrual blood is considered to render the woman impure and she is "banished" during her period. During this time, she is subjected to various prohibitions, such as not engaging in sexual intercourse. Some people believe that during her period, she is even forbidden to be seen in public for fear that her very presence will cause a disaster – the bread will not rise, the wine will turn sour, and the crops will wither. The connotation of blood is disaster, according to the belief that blood symbolizes the sin that still exists in our world.

Blood in Christianity

ccording to the New Testament, Jesus saved humanity by sacrificing his life. Prior to his crucifixion, he partook of a last supper with his disciples, and the wine they drank symbolized his blood that was about to be spilled. The church elders had to fight against the interpretation of this supper so that it would not encourage pagan acts, such as human sacrifice or various kinds of cannibalistic rites. Indeed, in the year 777, the leader of a German tribe succeeded in conquering a neighboring Saxon tribe. Several years later, he announced that not only had he succeeded in forcing the pagan Saxons to undergo baptism, but he had also put to death those who had confused pagan beliefs with Christian rituals. However, despite these precautionary measures, blood in the Christian world was linked to supernatural powers that formed the infrastructure for the development of the belief in the existence of vampires.

Reincarnation

The belief in reincarnation – or life after death – also links Christianity to the vampire myth. The body, which is nothing but a simple substantial covering, decays, while the soul continues to live in another world, waiting for renewal. The souls of sinners can be saved even before their death, as long as they manage to redeem themselves. The souls of the sinners who were not redeemed on their deathbed by a Christian priest or who were not buried in a Christian ceremony (people who committed suicide or were excommunicated) would continue to be reborn in the world, deprived of eternal rest. According to the Christian belief, these are "souls who are immersed in pain", belonging neither to the world of the dead nor to the world of the living. However, unlike vampires, these souls are not disguised by the body that covers them, and for that reason are not vulnerable.

Vampires from the Middle Ages to the modern era

*I*n the 11th century, many witches and physicians would drain the blood of young girls in order to cure various diseases and also to retard the aging processes. The origin of this procedure resides in the belief that young blood is extremely valuable and has the ability to fortify and enhance life. At the same time, the belief in the existence of vampires increased, gradually intensifying until it reached its peak in the 15th century. These were the centuries in which superstitions and preconceptions prevailed.

The first testimonies to the existence of vampires that have been found came from the 11th century. In the journal of a Frenchman by the name of Jacques Albine Simon Colin de Plancy, it was found that according to a report drawn up in 1031 by the bishop of Cahors, a city in the center of France, the body of a knight was found lying at a short distance from his grave. In the 12th century, Latin texts written by two Augustinian monks were found in England, according to which the graves of dead people were opened following various rumors, and bloodstains were found on the bodies. The terrible spell could only be annulled after driving swords through the corpses and burning them. A possible explanation for this stated that during that time, the dead were buried in a hurry – sometimes without ensuring that they were actually dead – in order to avoid the spread of epidemics. When the coffins were opened, it seemed as if the dead people had suffered inside them and had tried to escape from them. It did not take a great deal of imagination, therefore, to believe that these corpses had turned into vampires. This is how the belief in the existence of vampires began to be assimilated and entrenched in the collective 14th-century imagination, especially in Central and Eastern Europe.

The belief became official in the second half of the 16th century, in no small part due to the Reformation movement, which was based on the Roman Catholic faith. Martin Luther (1483-1546) himself related to the phenomenon and in this way transformed the myth into an official belief. The theologian Louis Lauwater claimed that the revenants, who until then had been considered to be the messengers of Satan, were nothing but demons. He said that this belief was based on nothing less than the writings of the king of Scotland, James VI, Demonology .

In the 17th century, the belief in the existence of vampires spread southward toward Albania, Bulgaria and Greece, and eastward toward Austro-Hungary and the Russian Empire. It flourished in Eastern Europe even more than in Western Europe. The reasons for this were demographic, social and theological. Since the end of the 16th century, the countries of Eastern Europe had been poor and isolated, especially the mountainous ones, and the intellectual and humanistic discoveries of the Renaissance did not reach them. Most of the population was still ignorant and illiterate, and superstitions were transmitted orally by travelers who found these unenlightened countries to be fertile ground for them. Moreover, in the Catholic countries – Germany, southern France, northern Italy, Spain and Portugal – the Roman church was fighting against superstitions, while in the Protestant countries such as Britain and Switzerland, the church spread propaganda against witches. In the East, the Byzantine Orthodox Church was far more forgiving in its attitude toward superstitions, and even included some of them in its texts.

Although a single colers who found these unenlightened countries to be fertile ground for them. Moreover, in the Catholic countries – Germany, southern France, northern-rrence had been reported in so many places that in eastern Prussia an order was given to open all the graves in order to check on the coffins.

While the term vampire had been used in different ways it was now widespread mainly in its Latin use – vampirus. At the beginning of the 18th century, the "vampire" was characterized as a dead person who comes to life and is not a ghost, who leaves his grave at night in order to suck the blood of live people in order to prolong his existence, and whose victims become vampires themselves after their death. However, in the German culture, people preferred to relate to the vampire as a shadow or reflection that symbolized a lost soul. Wild imagination attributed werewolf teeth to the image of the vampire, and the teeth were actually used for sucking, not for biting. Some people turned the bat into a kind of incarnation of a vampire – thanks to Georges-Louis Leclair de Bouffon, who, in 1760, named the bat that sucked the blood of animals and cattle in Central America a "vampire". In fact, the legendary vampire could transmogrify into various animals – from spiders to butterflies – and even appear as fog or pieces of straw.

The wise man who seeks pleasure discovers that there is " a number of desire levels", then he abandons both Virtue and Vice, becoming a Kiaista. Riding his desire shark, he crosses the ocean of duality and dives into self-love.

Austin Osman Spare

The vampire from Berwick

The chronicles of William Neuberg of 1196 contain a text about the vampire of Berwick. It dealt with a rich man who lived in Berwick in northern England, near the Scottish border, in the 12th century. After his death, the villagers reported that they had seen his body wandering the city streets at night, causing the dogs to howl the whole night through. Fearing that he would attack the residents, the people of the city decided to exhume the body and burn it. Afterwards, the wandering ceased, but in its place a serious epidemic afflicted the inhabitants of Berwick and caused the deaths of hundreds of them. Then they believed that there was an effect caused by the presence of the vampire...

The trial of Giles de Raisse

I n 1440, the trial of one of Jeanne d'Arc's guards took place in France. He had retired from his job and devoted himself to alchemy on his estate in the south of France. According to the description in Karl Hausmann *La Bas*'s 1891 book, de Raisse was none other than a completely authentic vampire, who, during his attempts to discover the secrets of alchemy and turn substances into gold, did not recoil from brutal and terrible ways of killing close to 300 innocent children…

Prince Tepes

*T*he prince of Wallachia, Vlad Tepes, lived from 1431 to 1476. He ruled the ancient kingdom of Wallachia and became its national hero after fighting courageously to liberate the kingdom from the Ottoman invaders. Except that Tepes was also a bloodthirsty warrior who killed thousands of people along the way simply for pleasure. Fifteenth-century German texts relate that Tepes' favorite mode of killing was by tearing his victims into shreds. Tepes is described as one of the most bloodthirsty warriors in history, and was called "Dracula" after his father Dracul, which means devil or dragon. His legendary image served as a source of great inspiration for the vampire myth, particularly for the Irish writer Bram Stoker, who wrote the immortal and successful novel, *Dracula*, hundreds of years later.

Countess Elizabeth (Erzsebet) Bathory

C ountess Elizabeth Bathory is well-known as a "genuine" vampire because in 1611 she was accused of abducting and torturing to death 80 to 200 helpless young girls who lived not far from her castle on a hill close to the Carpathian mountains. Although the accusation in question was real and not a supernatural phenomenon, there were people who claimed that Bathory would drink the blood of her victims and immerse herself in a bath filled with their blood in order to preserve her youth.

The story of Elizabeth Bathory is truly shocking. She was born in 1560 to George and Anna Bathory, in the region of Hungary that would later become what is known today as Slovakia. In her childhood, she was a very angry child and had a stormy and uncontrollable temperament. She lived with her family in Cachtrice Castle, near the town of Vishine, a region in which lengthy battles between the Turkish and the Austrian armies took place during the era when large portions of Europe were under the control of the Ottoman Empire. There were many religions and languages in this region. Elizabeth's family belonged to the new wave of religious Protestants who opposed the Roman Catholic tradition.

In 1571, her cousin Stephan became the prince of Transylvania, and afterwards claimed the Polish crown. He was known as the most effective ruler of his time, since he planned to unite Europe against the Turkish Empire. When Elizabeth was only 14, she had a brief affair with one of the peasants in the region and became pregnant. Her family placed her in seclusion until the birth of the child, since they did not want the family of her future fiancé, Count Ferenc Nadasdy, to find out. Indeed, about a year later, in 1575, she married Nadasdy, and they lived in Sarvar Castle, her husband's estate.

Nadasdy was a soldier who was away from home for long periods of time. It was during his absence that Bathory's evil career began to flourish. It began when she imposed a harsh reign of terror on the employees of her castle, especially on the young girls who served her. While such conduct was common in those days among people of the upper classes, Bathory's cruelty, as it turned out later, was boundless. Not only did she punish those who did not obey her, but she enjoyed torturing them and bringing about their deaths. She did this, for instance, by sticking pins into sensitive places beneath their fingernails or by taking them outside naked during the winter and pouring water over them until they froze.

And so, while Bathory devoted herself, among other things, to the study of black magic, her husband would participate in some of her torture sessions during his brief furloughs. Some people say that he even taught her new methods of torture. Once she took one of the maids outside during the summer, smeared honey over her naked body, and let the bees and other insects swarm over her and sting her.

In 1604, Nadasdy died in battle, and Elizabeth moved to her manor in Cachtice. There, in Slovakia, the most ghastly deeds took place. With the help of her servant Turko, it is said that she abducted innocent girls, incarcerated them in her castle and tortured them slowly to death. Over time, the couple improved and added three more servants to the team. After scores of cases of missing young girls were reported in the region of Bathory's castle, the rumors began to spread, until her cousin led policemen and soldiers to her castle. They found Bathory and her henchmen at the climax of one of their blood orgies. Scores of corpses of young women were found there, as well as dozens of tortured women who were locked up and bleeding to death. Many other prisoners were awaiting a similar fate.

In 1610, Bathory and her servants were imprisoned and put on trial. They were accused of killing at least 650 girls. At the end of the trial, Bathory's sentence was commuted because of her late husband's ties with the royal family. Her servants and assistants were executed forthwith. The judges sentenced her to incarceration and solitary confinement in a closed room in her castle until the day she died, with no windows or doors, only a tiny window for food and a little air. She only survived three years in her jail, and died in 1614.

The castle was abandoned and for years it was believed to be cursed. Since that affair, numerous rumors and legends emerged, such as the belief that the servants rose up from their graves and continued their appalling deeds after their death. Bathory was also accused of being a werewolf or a vampire after one of the witnesses at the trial testified that she bit the flesh of one of the girls she was torturing. She was accused of using the blood of her victims and bathing in it in order to preserve her youth. Indeed, Elizabeth Bathory was considered to be a very beautiful and attractive woman.

Most of the evidence from Bathory's trial was sealed and its publication prohibited, since the Hungarian government was horrified by the ghastly publicity it would engender. However, a century later, a priest by the name of Turoczy located copies of the trial documents and collected stories from people in the Cachice region. He documented all the evidence in a book that was later included in Hungarian history. In this book, he suggested the possibility that Bathory bathed in the blood of her victims. His book was published in 1720, when the belief in the existence of vampires was already widespread in Europe. Turoczy described how Bathory's blood lust began. It happened when one of her young servants was combing her hair and accidentally hurt her. Elizabeth slapped her hard across the face and blood spurted out of the girl's mouth and soiled Bathory's hands. She rubbed her hands together, and then saw that they looked younger. According to the story, that is when Bathory's quest for the blood of young virgins began.

Although the story of her bathing in blood is metaphorically compatible with the image of the vampire, Bathory was not legally accused of being a vampire, but rather of being a cold-blooded torturer and murderer of helpless and innocent women. Over the years, she became one of the sources of inspiration for many horror stories and movies, mainly in the 20th century. Bram Stoker himself, the creator of *Dracula* in 1897, read about Elizabeth Bathory in *The Book of Werewolves* by Evin Brin-Gold (1865), and some people claim that as a result of her influence, Stoker decided to transfer the plot of his book to the region in Transylvania in which Elizabeth Bathory's castle was located, and in which she performed her grisly deeds.

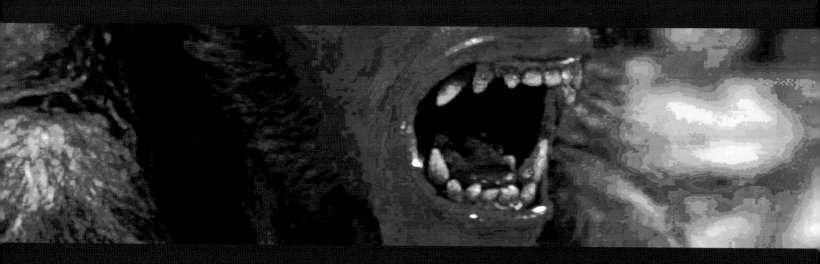

Vrykolakas

The word originates from the Slavic language and means werewolf, that is, a person who can turn into a wolf-like creature. Some 3,000 cases of werewolves were registered in Europe between 1520 and the 17th century, mainly in France, Serbia, Bohemia and Hungary. That is the result of an official investigation conducted by the Roman Catholic church. It involved testimonies of people pertaining to vrykolakas – a bloodthirsty monstrous creature, a person that turned into a wolf-like creature after his death. This creature fed on the blood of living people. In fact, it is another version of the vampire, except that the word *vampire* was not yet known.

Bruxa / Bruja / Strega

Bruxa is a Portuguese witch (bruxo is a wizard). The belief in the bruxa was based on pagan beliefs and on her satanic properties. In 12th-century Portugal, the beliefs in spells proliferated, and although the government did a great deal to quash them, it was unsuccessful, and the bruxa became the witch that sucked the blood of infants and entered the category of the vampires of the Western world. The belief stated that the bruxa appears mainly as a duck, a mouse, a goose, a dove or an ant, and she conducted her activity between midnight and two o'clock in the morning. In every region, the witches would congregate at the crossroads on Tuesdays and Fridays and worship Satan, from whom they derived their evil powers, as well as the "evil eye". To this day, Tuesday and Friday have a negative connotation in Portuguese folklore.

In order to protect oneself against the bruxa and keep her away from the children, it was necessary to stick a metal nib into the ground or place a pair of scissors under the pillow. Furthermore, certain Portuguese words could keep her away, and as a final precaution, garlic was inserted into the children's clothes so that they would not be abducted by the bruxa.

Bruja is the name for a witch in Spanish. It describes a living person, generally a woman, who appears in the form of various animals and attacks infants. In Mexico, the bloodsucking witch was called the tlahuelpuchi. The name for the same witch in Italy is strega.

An eyewitness testimony

An eyewitness testimony, as it appeared in a report, tells about the Hungarian Peter Plogojovitz – the Hungarian who ostensibly turned into a vampire after his death in 1725 and caused the death of over ten people in the village of Kizolova, in the region of today's Serbia. In that year, Plogojovitz was seen by German soldiers who were stationed in the village and testified that they had seen him wandering around alive ten weeks after his death, even though he had been buried in accordance with the rites and the tradition of the times.

At the same time, nine cases of dead people – both young and old – were discovered in the village. They had died after suffering from no more than a 24-hour illness. Each of them declared, before dying, that Plogojovitz himself, who had died two and a half months previously, had appeared at their deathbed. According to the report, the witnesses related that Plogojovitz himself lay down on their dying bodies and strangled them to death. In addition, it is written that Plogojovitz's wife herself testified that after his death, her husband appeared and demanded his shoes. After she had given them to him, he left the village of Kizolova.

The writer who transcribed the testimonies added that as a result of these rumors, it was decided to open Plogojovitz's grave. He relates that he himself and the priest were asked to serve as witnesses to the exhumation ceremony. Although he told the inhabitants that these rumors were unfounded and there was no need to open the grave, the villagers all threatened to leave because they were afraid that if the situation remained as it was, they were liable to be killed by the evil spirit of Plogojovitz. For this reason, states the writer, I left for the village of Kizolova in order to examine the body.

The grave was indeed opened and the astonished writer described how fresh the corpse appeared to him. The hair and nails had grown, and new skin covered the pale skin of the dead person. All of the other organs were intact, just as if they were alive. In addition, signs of fresh blood could be discerned in the dead man's mouth. This matched the testimonies of the people who had died and had stated that Plogojovitz had sucked their blood.

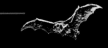
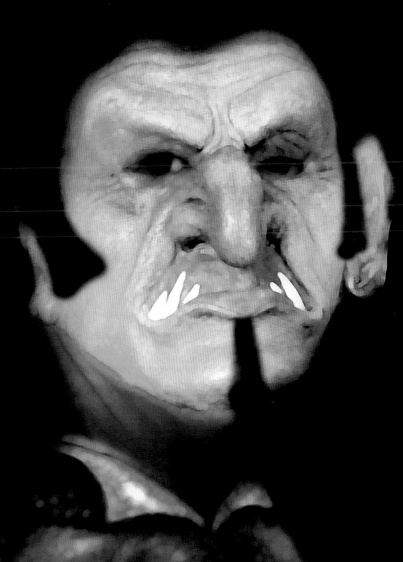

In the light of what they had seen, the villagers sharpened a wooden stake and drove it into Plogojovitz's chest, right into the heart of the dead man. Blood ran from his mouth and ears when they did this. Afterwards, the corpse was burned and the ashes scattered. The written testimony does not mention Plogojovitz's character, but it is clear that he was a simple peasant who did not belong to the aristocracy.

In this written testimony, vampirism was presented as a plague, and in fact the rapid consecutive deaths of the nine people were reminiscent of death as a result of a plague. As rational people, we must deny this phenomenon, but for the peasants, it was a real belief. The fact that death attacked the village and killed people one after the other within a day, in addition to the fear that the revenant could destroy all the living people in the village, was enough for them.

From then on, the power of the imagination remained buried in human memory. This model of the vampire who is in habit of leaving his grave at night, manifesting himself to his victims, and sucking their blood or strangling them, became extremely widespread and familiar. Also, the fact that the dead person did not appear to be dead when he was exhumed from his grave, and that blood was seen on his mouth, reinforces the assumption that he was a vampire. In the official report documenting the case of Plogojovitz, the term vampire (Vanpir in German) was used for the first time. In this way, Peter Plogojovitz's place as one of the modern vampires of human history was determined.

The next case involved an entire village that was infected with a "plague". For this reason, the case captured the attention of the authorities, who were forced to send official investigators to the place. These investigators wrote the following report, which was signed in the presence of many witnesses.

The report described a man by the name of Arnold Paul, who, in 1726, died as a result of a broken neck when he fell from a crop wagon. According to the report, it was found that a vampire was roaming around the village of Medvegia and was responsible for the deaths of many people by sucking their blood. The investigators were sent to the Serbian village where they discovered that Paul had been molested by a vampire while he was still alive, and in order to free himself from him, he would eat dirt from another vampire's grave and roll himself in vampire blood. Twenty or thirty days after Paul's death, several people filed complaints, claiming that they had been harassed by Paul. Four of them also died. As a result of these testimonies, Paul's grave was opened at the recommendation of one of the witnesses to an identical phenomenon in another place, and Paul's corpse was found intact with fresh blood flowing from its eyes, mouth and ears. The dead man's shirt and coffin were covered with blood. His nails and skin had grown once again. The eyewitnesses immediately understood that it was a vampire lying in front of them, and, as was customary, sharpened a wooden stake and drove it through his heart. A sigh issued from him when he delivered his soul and died for the second time. Afterwards, his body was burned, and the same day his ashes were thrown back into his grave. However, some people who claimed that all those who had been attacked by him would eventually become vampires themselves. It was also said that Paul sucked the blood of the cattle in the village, and anyone who ate the flesh of the cattle would also become tainted.

The case of Arnold Paul caused an uprising following the police report, in which the regimental field surgeon, Johannes Fluckinger, wrote: "Visum et repertum (seen and revealed)". It was authorized by many military clerks and physicians. The report was sent to the Austrian consulate in Belgrade, published in 1732, and sparked a great deal of curiosity. The Austrian emperor, Charles VI, followed the affair closely, and the French king, Louis XV, consulted at length with his advisors regarding the details of the report. Following these two affairs, the phenomenon continued to spread all over Europe – this time accompanied by the term *vampyre*. In the same year, the term was first used in France, while it appeared in English for the first time in an article in the *London Times*, which described the case in detail.

An academic investigation of the phenomenon (18ᵗʰ century)

T he belief in the existence of vampires also reached academic circles and universities. The rumors and gossip were documented in the 18th century and investigated mainly by doctorate holders and other scholars. In 1679, Philip Rohr wrote a research study about the dead, entitled: "Dissertatio Historica-Philosophica de Masticatione Mortuorum", in which he tried to explain the phenomenon of the sound of the dead chewing in their graves. This book sparked a massive controversy between those who accepted Roher's supernatural explanation and those who opposed it in the name of logic and came out against ignorance and superstition. In 1728, Michel Ranft published a book entitled "De Masticatione Mortuorum in Tumulis Liber", and he also wrote about the dead moving around in their coffins. His conclusion stated that even if the dead can affect the living, they cannot appear and exist after their death, and that the devil does not have the power to enter the bodies of the dead. Two other publications that caused repercussions were John Christian

Stock's 1732 article, "Dissertatio Physica de Cadauveribus Sanguisugis", about the physical nature of bloodsucking skeletons, and Jonathan Heinrich Zoff's 1733 manuscript, "Dissertatio de Vampiris Serviensibus", according to which vampires exist only in dreams and under the devil's influence.

Dom Augustin Calmet

om Augustin Calmet was the best-known vampire researcher at the beginning of the 18th century. He was a French Roman Catholic biblical scholar whose comprehensive research did not allow the church to remain indifferent, especially in view of the fact that Calmet himself was a Benedictine monk who was known for his commentaries on the Bible. Calmet was born in Bréville, France, in 1672, and studied in a Benedictine monastery there. In 1688, he entered the order, and was ordained at age 24. Calmet studied philosophy and theology, and between 1707 and 1716, published texts and commentaries on the Bible, which turned him into one of the leading ecclesiastical scholars. In 1746, Calmet sought to tackle the vampire phenomenon, and conducted comprehensive research based on various reports and writings that he collected from Germany and particularly from Eastern Europe. The phenomenon was unknown in France and was not known to the scholarly community there until the beginning of the 18th century, and for this reason Calmet was impressed by it and by the testimonies he read, and believed that it would not make sense simply to ignore them or make them disappear. He included the various testimonies in his book, which was published in 1746, and while it was somewhat naive, it is of great interest to many historians, sociologists and anthropologists.

As a theologist, Calmert realized that the belief in the existence of vampires could have significant implications with regard to life after death. He decided that the phenomenon must be comprehended in the light of the view of the church, and collected as much evidence as possible from official documents, newspapers, eyewitnesses and travelers, and documented everything in his book, with the addition of his learned opinion on the subject. Calmet took all the explanations of the phenomenon into account, but even so, was unable to draw unequivocal conclusions because the reports supported the "natural" explanations for the undoubted existence of vampires, so he left the matter open. However, he wrote that "it is impossible not to relate to the widespread belief in these countries that these creatures have come directly from their graves and are capable of causing everything mentioned above."

It can actually be understood from his words that the existence of vampires was a result of evil doings. Although Calmet did not reach a single clear conclusion, he wrote in the third and final edition of his book that he was unable to conclude anything except that these creatures were people who had died and been buried, afterwards rising up from their graves in order to disturb the living by sucking their blood and causing them to die.

In this manner, in fact, the church confirmed, albeit unofficially, the existence of the phenomenon. Even if other important religious figures did not particularly encourage it, their serious attitude toward it reinforced the belief in it. In the generation following Calmet, he was attacked by many French intellectuals both inside and outside the church. Later on, he was attacked by Denis Diderot, in whose book, *L'Encyclopédie*, he warned against the phenomenon and reprimanded Calmet, but also related to it seriously. The satirist Voltaire related sarcastically to Calmet, and even the philosopher Jean-Jacques Rousseau related to the phenomenon in his letter to the archbishop of Paris, in which he demanded to know how the superstition had turned into such an all-encompassing belief. Now the term vampire was known to everyone by name, and was no longer the province of just a few.

Vampires in the age of reason

O nce belief was overcome by empirical science, according to which true knowledge can stand firmly against natural phenomena, and once the spread of epidemics through the continent of Europe diminished, the belief in the existence of vampires also began to wane. Since the end of the 18th century, after the topic was investigated and became controversial in the universities and among academics, especially in France and Germany, the reports of supernatural occurrences like these also decreased. With the advent of the 19th century, the Industrial Revolution brought new ways of life and greatly undermined the existence of superstitions. It created a new world in which there was no longer room for witches and imaginary creatures from the past.

The roots of the vampires were embedded deep in human history as a result of their being one of the products of the collective European mind. This monster was created prior to the age of reason, at a time when superstition prevailed, and now logic ruled that it had to disappear or become a museum exhibit. Actually, in the second half of the 18th century, very little was written about vampires. Having said that, in certain places – such as that little village in the Carpathian mountains, where it was still customary to open graves in order to search for traces of vampires – the belief persisted. Even though most of the readers of the new age press preferred to read about the century's new technological inventions, rationalism had still not eliminated the vampire legend.

Vampires in the literary culture

T he Romantic movement, which emerged as a reaction to the Industrial Revolution and came out against the new materialistic atmosphere, allowed for the nostalgia and charm of the past. This literary movement was established in Germany as a result of a struggle against the domination of emotion by reason. The Romantics thought that the individual's emotions must be expressed before the collective rational expression. The Romantic movement encouraged the return to the times in which people still believed in miracles, and the old world served as a greater inspiration for them than the cold new world.

Thus the vampire phenomenon began to filter into a new domain: the domain of literary imagination. At the end of the century, the second generation of English Romanticism was born. It displayed a great deal of interest in the supernatural, and the vampire legend was revived in the English Romantic poetry of the time. The vampire now became a fable and a symbol. In the poems of Gottfried August Burger (1773) and of Johann Wolfgang von Goethe (*Die Baut von Corinth*, 1797), the vampire became a metaphor for lost passion, when it was described as a young man or woman who returned from the world of the dead. Ballads about seductive vampires were written (such as John Keats' *La Belle Dame sans Merci* as well as *Lemia*), and the question of whether the vampire protagonist drank the blood of his victims or not was not the focus of the preoccupation with the phenomenon. The important thing was that the vampire symbolized the possibility of returning to life from the world of the dead, and by means of the myth, the poets were able to supply their readers with the sado-masochistic aspect of the relations between vampire and victim. This served as an example of the kind of relations that existed between couples in fantastic literature to this day. In this way, too, the **femme fatale** was born – the seductive woman who represented something beyond the Romantic period, and whose myth was preserved until the beginning of the 20th century.

Lord Byron and the vampires

L ord George Gordon Byron was actually the first writer to write a story about the modern vampire in English. Byron was born in London in 1788 and was taken to Aberdeen in Scotland by his mother during his childhood. There, he led a deprived childhood after his father frittered away his entire fortune. Luckily for him, after the death of his cousin and great-uncle, he became a wealthy English lord. He went to study at Cambridge University and published his first book of poetry in 1806, followed by the second one in 1807. A year later, he received his degree and then became a member of the House of Lords. In 1812, his publications made him famous.

A year later, he published a poem called "The Giaour", which was about vampires. In this poem, he displayed his familiarity with the Greek *vrykolakas* vampires. In 1816, Byron separated from his wife after numerous love affairs, and, accompanied by the young writer and physicist, John Polidori, arrived in Geneva, where he stayed in the Villa Diodati. In this villa, the two met Percy Shelley and his wife, Mary. One evening, they sat together and read ghost stories. When it was over, Byron made a suggestion: Each person present should write a ghost story of his or her own. The intellectuals who were present in the room agreed to the suggestion with alacrity. That same night, Mary Shelley-Godwin thought up the novel *Frankenstein*, which, over the years, would become a milestone in English vampire literature. In contrast to his wife, Percy Shelley lost interest in the matter and wrote nothing, while Lord Byron scribbled a brief idea in his notebook.

After Polidori and Byron left the villa, friction and tension erupted between them, leading to a parting of the ways. One day, in 1819, Byron came across the story, "The Vampire", which had been published in the *New Monthly Magazine*. To his astonishment, he saw that he was featured as the writer. After making some brief inquiries, it transpired that John Polidori had written the story, but had based it on the idea Lord Byron had scribbled in his notebook that evening at the Villa Diadoti in Geneva.

This story was the first fictional prose relating to vampires. The vampire became a literary hero that was characterized in prose writing for the first time. In the tension between fantasy and reality, the vampire sucked not only blood, but also the physical energy of the readers – the energy that controlled their mental and physical functions. Slowly but surely, the vampire turned into the object of their passion.

The story features a vampire protagonist – whom Byron had thought up in the villa – while the other protagonists were the fruit of Polidori's imagination and had different names. He turned the vampire into Lord Ruthven, a cynical seducer who oddly enough resembled Lord Byron himself. The story was published in England in April 1819 and was adapted for the theater and staged by Charles Nodier in 1820 as well as by Alexander Dumas in 1852. Thanks to Lord Byron's idea, the vampire filtered through from poetry to literature, and Polidori's book became very important in the history of vampire literature. The new aristocratic vampire served as a great inspiration for the Irish writer, Bram Stoker, and for his immortal vampire in the novel *Dracula*. The story was translated and published with huge success, and even though Polidori and Byron tried to correct the distortions, it was too late, and *The Vampire* was published.

England and its affection for vampire protagonists

Until 1850, vampire literature was very popular, but after that those texts began to bore the public throughout the world and their quality declined. Only in Victorian England did the insatiable thirst for horror story and supernatural fantasies continue. This public need was nothing but a natural continuation of the national tradition in Britain, which was always a country of ghosts and horror stories. Although the Industrial Revolution had dampened this tradition, the demand for these stories did not cease. It is possible that they now served as a creative and liberating alternative to the new concepts of money, religion and income, and these horror stories were sold to the broad English public for pennies in cheap magazines that were available to all.

Carmilla

The novel *Carmilla* was written by the Irish writer, Joseph Sheridan Le Fanu and published in 1871. He had been preceded by famous writers such as Charles Dickens and Lord Lytton, who espoused the fantastic idea when they included it in their books of 1859 and responded to the needs of the British public (Dickens in his book *The Enchanted House* and Lord Lytton in his book, *The Witches and the Wizards*). These novels serve as the basis for the appearance of the novel Carmilla, which now revitalized the tremendous vampire tradition. Le Fanu succeeded in providing his readers with a great deal of pleasure and became an additional source of inspiration for Bram Stoker's famous novel, *Dracula*, which consolidated the vampire myth of the modern age.

Dracula

*B*ram Stoker was a stage manager and director of the Royal Theatre in London. After the theater failed, Stoker turned his hobby into a profession and began to write full-time in order to earn a living. Stoker had been influenced by fantastic literature when he was still a youth, and had read a great deal of vampire literature, including the well-known novel *Carmilla*. Now he was determined to write his own vampire story, and to this end, began to examine the phenomenon and the legend in depth. This included delving into the secrets of black magic and reading a guide to the culture of Transylvania by Emily Gerard.

He drew his inspiration for the shaping of his protagonist from Arminius Vambéry, a professor of Eastern languages at Budapest University, who was famous for his historical research of mid-European folklore. During a visit to London, Vambéry told Stoker about the true life of Dracula, the terrible Vlad Tepes, and the writer, who relished the exotic sound of the name, decided to us it as the name of the protagonist in his book.

In 1897, Dracula appeared for the first time, without the first chapter, which had been eliminated by the writer. This chapter was published separately by his widow in 1914 as a novella entitled "Dracula's Guest", which featured a female character that was no doubt inspired by *Carmilla*.

The plot of the novel *Dracula* is known to many people not least as a result of the movie versions it engendered. The protagonist, Jonathan Harker, is sent to Transylvania to inspect a businessman by the name of Count Dracula who wishes to buy property in England. During the course of the plot, Harker discovers Dracula's terrible secret: he is actually a revenant, a vampire that rises from his grave at night in order to quench his thirst for human blood. The courageous young man tracks Dracula's crimes, and thus begins the battle between good and evil. Initially, Dracula chooses the friend of Harker's fiancée, Lucy, as his victim, and she dies while he is sucking her blood. Eventually, Harker, Mina, Professor Van Helsing and the American, Morris, subdue the terrible vampire. The absolute end of Dracula only occurs after Harker cuts his throat and Morris drives a knife through his heart. Dracula turns into dust, and Mina – the next victim – is saved from death.

The novel enables the reader to follow the protagonist step by step, from his first encounter with the horror until his war with and subsequent victory over evil. As a novel, *Dracula* was a special genre that succeeded in preserving the atmosphere of the gothic novel (the mystery within the dark castle), while it was actually located in the modern world of the end of the 19th century, with part of the novel even taking place in London. *Dracula* was the first book of its kind to succeed in creating an authentic atmosphere. In order to attain this atmosphere, the author spent many days in the British Museum in his quest for the history of vampires; he researched the geography of Transylvania and the cultural folklore. Like the fathers of the vampires, Stoker's protagonist, too, had no reflection, shunned garlic and Christian symbols, came to life only at night and was nourished by human blood.

To this day, *Dracula* is considered the masterpiece of fantastic literature. It has been translated into numerous languages and has been published worldwide. In fact, Dracula was the mythical vampire figure of the 20th century. However, even though it met the needs of the Victorian public and succeeded in undermining the British values of harmony and order, Dracula was not a sweeping public success.

It was actually the visual dimension that caused *Dracula*'s popularity to skyrocket: theater and cinema. In June 1924, *Dracula* was staged as a play for the first time in the theater in Derby, England, directed by Hamilton Dean, twelve years after the death of Stoker. The vampire protagonist was dressed in an evening suit and a black cloak. Three years later, the play was transferred to London, where it was so successful that it crossed the Atlantic that same year and was staged on Broadway. From there, the road to historic success was extremely short.

Dracula in the cinema

The actor, Bela Lugosi, was the first Dracula on the Broadway stage, but he soon went on to play this role on the screen, where he turned the character into a legend. The first "talking picture" about Dracula was screened in 1931 and marked the beginning of the modern myth about the character. However, it was not the first screen Dracula. In 1922, a silent movie about Dracula had been produced by a German director (F. W. Murnau), but practically failed to make any impression. Only nine years later was the modern myth born in Hollywood.

The movie *Dracula* reached the American public during one of the most difficult times it had ever known: the Great Depression. The personality of the protagonist represented the hatred and anger of millions of people in the wake of the financial crisis. Lugosi, with his Hungarian accent, his pale appearance and sickly smile, succeeded in portraying this better than anybody else. Following in his footsteps, similar movies were made, and these were popular until the end of World War II. This is how, alongside the American culture of "life as it's supposed to be" of the 1950s, the myth of Dracula spread overseas as well. Vampire movies were made in Italy, Spain, Mexico and even the Philippines.

 Over the years, the face of Dracula changed: In 1958, he was played by the English actor, Christopher Lee. Subsequently he was played by other actors who did not resemble the legendary Bela Lugosi. Lee created a new image of a vampire: a tall, handsome man in his fifties, with gray hair and a respectable aristocratic appearance. Lee acted in many Dracula movies, until he starred in a comic parody of himself in 1976. An entire generation completely identified Christopher Lee with the character he portrayed, so that most of the actors after him simply preferred to imitate him.

Leo Allatius

Leo Allatius was the first modern author to write a vampire novel. He was a Greek vampire researcher who was born on the island of Chios in 1586, moved to Rome, where he studied in a college, and then returned to his island in order to serve as the Catholic bishop's assistant. Later, he settled in Italy, where he studied medicine and worked in the Vatican library for many years. His dream was to effect the reunification of the Roman and Greek churches.

In 1645, Allatius wrote a book in which he listed the beliefs that prevailed among the inhabitants of Greek. Quite a few chapters were devoted to the Greek vampire tradition. He described the Greek vampires, the *vrykolakas*, as corpses that had been snatched by demons, and he used them in order to write the Greek church's procedures for getting rid of them. In his book, Allatius also mentioned his own opinion regarding the existence of vampires, and in fact, the moment he accepted their presence and existence, he dropped the subject. He continued working in the Vatican library, and was appointed its director in 1661. He died in 1669. His book actually contributed to strengthening the tie between vampires and the belief in them that prevailed in 17th-century Greek culture and even before.

Vampires in Bulgaria

*B*ulgaria is the oldest region of Slavic settlement. It is situated south of Romania, between the Black Sea and the Mediterranean. In the seventh century AD, the Bulgarian tribes reached the region and joined the Slavic tribes that lived there. The Bulgarian tribes constituted a small minority, and eventually adopted the Slavic language. Christianity reached the region in the ninth century, after Pope Nicholas I sent missionaries to Bulgaria and made it into a state under the hegemony of Rome. When the Bulgarian ruler, Boris-Michael, was baptized, Bulgaria officially accepted Christianity.

In parallel to Christianity, another religious group developed in Bulgaria. This group consisted of the Bogomils, who had evolved from the Paulicians. They had fled from Asia after refusing to become Moslems. The Bogomils believed that the world was created by Satanael, the rejected son of God, and while the body was created by him, the soul came from God. Of course, the church did not permit the existence of this faith, and declared that the Bogomil faith was gnostic and pagan.

The church accused the Bogomils of being the source of the existence of the Slavic vampire. Naturally, this was untrue, because the vampire idea prevailed in other European countries as well, even though there were no Bogomils present.

The word **vampir** came to Western culture from the Slavic language, on loan from Russian, and was also known as **vipir** or **vepir**. In Bulgaria it was believed that the spirits of the dead set out on their journey 40 days after death, and joined new life. However, if the burial was been performed properly, the deceased would never be able to go to the next world.

The Bulgarian custom dictated that the family was responsible for preparing the deceased for burial and they had to wash the corpse thoroughly. At the same time, it was forbidden for a dog or a cat to come anywhere near the place – not even for their shadow to fall on the corpse prior to burial. However, even if all these conditions were met, the deceased was still liable to turn into a vampire, especially if he had died a violent death.

In other Slavic countries, it was in fact other deceased persons who were candidates for becoming vampires: the ones who had been excommunicated by the community and ostracized, drunks, thieves, murderers, and of course, witches.

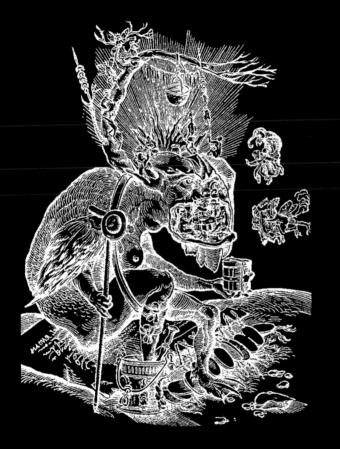

Throughout Bulgaria, many stories were told about dead people who came back to life in the form of vampires, living in villages and even marrying and having children. In other words, the prevalent belief was that the common Bulgarian vampire lived as an ordinary person during the day, and only at night set off on his bloodthirsty mission.

Another Bulgarian vampire was called *obur* by the Gaugaz people (Bulgarians who spoke Gaugazi). This name was borrowed from Turkish. According to the Gaugaz, the vampire had two additional properties: his voice sounded like the noise of firecrackers, and he could move objects from one place to another without touching them.

The *ustrel* was another vampire-like creature in Bulgaria, and it was actually nothing more than the spirit of a child who had been born on a Saturday but had died before being baptized. On the ninth day after its burial, so it was believed, the spirit found its way out of the grave, attacked cattle and sheep and drank their blood. After spending the whole night in its revels, the ustrel returned to its grave before dawn. Ten days later, it apparently became strong enough and no longer needed to return to its grave. Instead, it found a place where it could rest during the day, such as between the horns of a deer or between the legs of a milch-cow. The Bulgarians believed that the ustrel was capable of attacking an entire herd, beginning its rampage on the fattest of the animals. It was liable to attack five animals in a single night, and if one of them was found cut and wounded the next day, it was proof that it had been killed by the ustrel vampire. This is how the mysterious death of sheep or cows in Bulgaria was explained in the Middle Ages.

In order to overcome the phenomenon, the owner of the herd would hire the services of a vampire hunter, *vampirdzhija*, a special person with the ability to see the ustrel and remove any doubt about its existence. The moment it was identified by the vampire hunter, the latter would perform a special ritual in order to get rid of the vampire. According to the ritual, it was customary to extinguish all sources of fire in the village on the Saturday morning and the inhabitants had to walk to the nearest crossroads, where they set up logs for a bonfire. Two bonfires were lit, and the herd was trapped between them. Then, as the belief went, the vampire was forced to fall off the body of the animal to which it was clinging and remain at the crossroads, where it would be devoured by wolves. Before the bonfires were put out, one of the inhabitants would return to the village with the fire and light all the fires in the houses once more.

The other well-known vampires would be dispatched by driving the traditional wooden stake through their hearts. In Bulgaria, another special method of getting rid of vampires was common. An expert called a *djadajii* would carry a Christian icon on him – a picture of Jesus, Maria or one of the saints – and wait for the appearance of the vampire. When he saw him, he would use the icon to chase the vampire into a bottle that contained his favorite food. The bottle would be sealed and thrown into the fire.

In the last decades of the century, the Bulgarian government published manifestos against the superstitions, as it called them, regarding the church and vampires. Only after the power of the church was suppressed did the power of the beliefs that prevailed in the villages also wane, and the legends about the existence of vampires ceased to be a part of the modern consensus.

Vampires in Australia

*T*he belief in vampires does not occupy an important place in Australian folklore. However, the Aboriginal culture features creatures by the name of *yara-ma-yha-who* that have properties similar to those of vampires. They are red and very short, with a big head and a large toothless mouth. They swallow their food whole. The tips of their fingers and toes are sharp and reminiscent of an octopus' arms. The yara-ma-yha-who live at the top of fig-trees, and in order to hunt their prey, sit there and wait until their victim takes refuge in the shade of the tree, and then fall on it and attack it. They pierce their victims with their hands and feet and suck their blood until the victims are left weak and helpless. The yara-ma-yha-who can also kill people. Afterwards, they come back to eat the corpse, and after drinking water, fall into a deep sleep. The victims that survive and have been captured by the yara-ma-yha-who gradually become short, their skin softens, their bodies become covered with hair, until they become one of the small mythical forest creatures.

Vampires in Africa

The Africans are not known for their belief in vampires. In spite of their elaborate and rich mythology, the people of Africa are not known as people who hold a belief in the existence of vampires. However, the researcher Montegue Summers, who investigated the phenomenon in Africa in 1920, found that a creature called an *obayifo* existed in the African tradition, and it actually closely resembled the vampire. This West African vampire is called by different names among the neighboring tribes in West Africa – for instance, *asiman* among the Dahomeans.

This creature takes the form of a wizard who lives inside the community. The process of becoming a wizard does not occur as a result of any kind of genetic link, nor can anyone ever know who among the people of the community will become such a wizard. Both the obayifo and the asiman have the power to leave their body at night and wander around in the form of a ball of shining light. Their aim is to attack people, especially children, and suck their blood. Unlike the European vampire, the African vampire/wizard is also vegetarian, that is, it likes to suck fruit and vegetable juices.

Another African creature whose properties are reminiscent of those of the vampire is the *asasabonsam*. This is a vampire-like monster that is an inseparable part of the folklore of Ghana in West Africa. This monster looks like a human being with iron teeth. It generally lives in the depths of the forest and the chances of running into it are very small, since it lives on the treetops, well hidden, and only its legs dangle down. Innocent passers-by are liable to be caught by the hooked feet of the asasabonsam and become its prey.

Another prevalent belief, mainly among the tribes living near the Niger River in the delta region, involved witches that would leave their houses at night in order to hold meetings with various demons with the aim of plotting the death of people. Of course, the deaths were perpetrated by sucking the blood of the victim, and was called "sucking the heart". In this case, however, the sucking was done in a sophisticated manner: the witch's skill was so great that the victim felt pain but did not understand what was causing it. In fact, the witchcraft was nothing more than a clever method of poisoning, and perhaps this is why it resembled the prevalent belief in Europe of the Middle Ages that stated that the cause of death after being sucked by a vampire was blood poisoning.

The African witches wait on the roofs of the huts at night, and with their magic powers, they practice witchcraft and attack their unwitting victim. The members of the Nigerian Yako tribe believed that these were bodiless witches that attacked people at night and sucked their blood. Victims of tuberculosis were the "witnesses" to this deed, and when a lifeless victim was found with a bleeding wound or blister, it was concluded that he had fallen into the hands of one of these witches.

They also believed that death was sometimes caused by the fact that the witches would lie with the victim, and in this they resembled the *succubus*, the seductive female demon in Western culture who appeared in various versions – from Lilith to the femme fatale. Perhaps this is the reason why mainly sterile women or spinsters were blamed for casting these spells, and they were punished by being burned to death.

Another well-known African vampire is known in three different versions in other places, but they are very similar to one another. The *loogaroo*, whose traces were found in Haiti; the *asema*, whose existence was believed in by the people of Surinam; and the *sukuyan* in Trinidad. These three vampires are virtually identical to those that were later found in France, Denmark and England, and it seems that they were brought to these countries by African slaves.

A researcher by the name of John L. Vellutini studied the phenomenon and published two papers about it, in which he claimed that in addition to the witchcraft in which the Africans believed, it was possible to find additional parallels to the Slavic vampire that is known in the Western world, such as the fact that the African witches were capable of transforming themselves into various animals. Vellutini also found that those witches would gather around a cauldron called a baisea at night. They concentrated all of the blood of their victims in this cauldron, since the blood contained the vital properties of the victims. However, anyone who looked inside the cauldron would see nothing but transparent water. The witches also had the power to revive dead people and capture departed spirits and turn them into ghosts that would continue to harass the relatives of the dead person.

Another similarity between the European vampire and the African one lies in the manner of eliminating it: In one of the tribes, they would get rid of the vampire/wizard by pulling its tongue out of its mouth and pinning it to its chin with a thorn. It was killed by means of a sharpened stake, just like in Eastern Europe. In Africa, too, it was sometimes customary (as a precaution) to sever the vampire's head from its body, to burn the body or to leave it to the predators in the forest. (In Europe it was customary to sprinkle its ashes in the forest.)

In order to ascertain whether the deceased was a witch or a vampire, it was customary to exhume the corpse and check whether it contained marks of blood and to what extent it had decayed or swollen. If a hole in the dirt surrounding a grave was found, the Africans believed that it was the grave of a wizard who would emerge at night from his grave in the form of a bat, a mouse, or any other small animal.

In Africa, people also believed in the existence of the *isithfuntela* – a kind of witches' assistant that followed the witches' orders. It looked like a zombie after the witches that captured it cut out its tongue and drove a stake through its brain. The zombie itself would sometimes attack and capture victims by hypnotizing them and then piercing their heads with a long nail.

Vellutini found another similarity: The African vampires, just like the European ones, were just simple people. The reason why they were captured by the witches and transformed into vampires was that before their death, they were excommunicated by the community and ostracized, or they had committed suicide. In Vellutini's opinion, the belief of the people of Africa in these acts of witchcraft spread throughout the world and contributed to the development of the myth.

Vampires in the ancient world – Mesopotamia

*I*n the 19th century, writings from the ancient land of Mesopotamia – known today as Iraq – were discovered, and after they had been translated, they exposed an elaborate mythology in which it was possible to identify a divine legend that is slightly reminiscent of the later Western vampires.

There were seven evil spirits. These spirits are reminiscent of the *ekimmu* spirits that Montegue Summers discovered in his research on traditions of the ancient world. This is the spirit of a person who was not buried, and the belief in the ekimmu is based on the netherworld – the next world that comes after this one. These spirits were not permitted to enter the next world, since they had died alone, and they were condemned to roam the earth. The difference between those ancient spirits and Western vampires lies in the fact that the spirits do not eat people and drink their blood while they wander the earth, as vampires do.

Later translations of the *Gilgamish Epic* attest to the fact that the ekimmu ultimately do enter the next world – except that it is the underworld. It would seem that Summers was very keen to find a resemblance between the ekimmu and the vampires, but the difference between them is considerable.

African-American vampires

A t the end of the 18th century and at the beginning of the 19th century, cases of traditional and well-known bloodsuckers were reported in the black communities of the United States.

One case was in Tennessee, where it was told that an old woman who had been seen to be in poor health for a long time suddenly began to make an amazing recovery, while the health of her children gradually deteriorated. The reason, of course, was that the old woman was in the habit of sucking the children's blood while they slept. Eventually, the children died, while their elderly mother lived a long life.

In Louisiana, people believed in the existence of the *fifollet* – a light that was seen hovering over the marshes at night, and whose source was the *succubus* (the traditional bloodsucking female demon). The prevalent belief was that the fifollet is none other than the soul of the deceased that was sent back to the earth by God as a punishment. Instead of doing penance, however, the fifollet chose to attack living people. The fifollet missed its target in most of its attacks, but when one of its victims fell into its hands, he became a bloodsucking vampire, especially of children's blood. Some people preferred to believe that the fifollet was none other than the departed soul of a child that died before being baptized.

In the modern age, there are very few occurrences of vampires in African American folklore. At the beginning and end of the 1970s, several black vampire movies appeared, the best-known of which was *Blacula* (1972), starring William Marshall. The movie, which enjoyed a certain degree of fame, was about Prince Mamuwalde. A year later, *Scream Blacula Scream* was filmed. In addition, a movie called *Alabama's Ghost* about a group of vampires fighting a ghost was made. The movie *Ganja and Hess* (1973) told the story of Dr. Hess Green, who became a vampire after he was stabbed by an ancient African dagger. In later movies, the black actresses, Teresa Graves and Grace Jones starred in the movies *Old Dracula* and *Vamps*, respectively.

Female vampires

*T*he vampire in literature and cinema was generally a male. He would swoop down on the woman, who, until the 1960s, played the limited role of the helpless victim. However, the ancient mythical vampires were in fact women, and it should be remembered that there are also later ladies who played an indispensable role in the formation of the modern vampire, as well as an important part in the understanding of the myth.

As stated above, the first vampires in most of the ancient cultures were women. In Greece it was the *lamiai*, in Malaysia the *langsuyar*, and for the Jews, it was *Lilith*. Each of the above beings had a mythical problem with pregnancy and birth. It was said about the *langsuyar* that after giving birth to a stillborn infant, she flew to the forest and in her grief made it her solitary home. It was her despair that caused her to go out and take revenge on pregnant women and infants, and many Malaysian women used magical symbols in order to protect their pregnancies and their infants against her. The lamiai and Lilith also inspired terror and dread in the hearts of pregnant women. Lilith, who became one of the most famous figures in Jewish folklore, was a stormy demon who is identified with the night. She could cause complications in pregnancy and birth, and she was the source of barrenness or miscarriage. According to the Jewish belief, Lilith was a member of a group of Sumerian vampires, which included *Lillu*, *Ardat Lili* and *Irdu Lili*. She is mentioned

in the *Gilgamish Epic* that was written in approximately 2000 BC, and there she is described as a barren woman whose breasts were dry. In the same epic, Lilith, the gorgeous girl with the feet of an owl, is described as someone who had fled from her home near the river in favor of the desert. The prophet Isaiah mentions Lilith in one of his prophesies in the Bible, when he prophesies that the earth will become a desert once more, and a sign of this will be when Lilith settles there and finds peace there ["…Lilith shall repose there and find her place of rest," Isaiah 34:14].

The next appearance of Lilith is in the Talmud, where she is mentioned as Adam's first wife. According to the story, an argument erupted between Lilith and Adam with regard to which of them would be in the dominant position during intercourse. After Adam insisted on lying on top of her, Lilith abandoned him and flew – with the help of her magic powers – to the Red Sea, the place where the demons resided. Among them she found many lovers, and also met three angels of God – Senoy, Sansenoy and Semangelof – and reached an agreement with them. She promised not to use her satanic powers against protected infants, which she would identify by means of an amulet bearing one of the names of the three angels.

It is also written in the Talmud that Lilith's failure to seduce Adam did not give her any rest. After he was expelled from the Garden of Eden with his second wife, Eve, Lilith attacked him with her demon friends. As a result, Adam and Eve spawned many demon offspring.

According to this legend, Lilith is more similar to a *succubus* – the seductive female demon in the Western tradition – than to a vampire. Jewish men were also warned about sleeping alone in their homes, for fear of being attacked by Lilith. Lilith's hatred of men was well known, and part of her revenge on them is her attack on children – the products of the male sexual act – by sucking the children's blood and strangling them.

The myth about Lilith crystallized in Jewish folklore mainly in the generations preceding the Christian age. Although little was written about it since the completion of the Talmud (in the sixth century AD), Lilith was

mentioned again in the Kabbala literature. In the *Book of the Zohar* – which is the most significant Kabbala text in existence – Lilith is described as a succubus that lived at night and mainly attacked infants that were born as the result of illicit sexual relations. In addition, it was believed that when children laugh in their sleep, it is not because they are dreaming an innocent dream, but rather because they are playing with Lilith and have in fact fallen victim to her.

The Kabbala flourished and spread, and so did the stories about Lilith. Among other things, Lilith was identified as the Queen of Sheba, but the interesting story goes that she was one of the two women who appeared before King Solomon. Each of the women claimed that she was the mother of the child, and no one could reach a decision in the matter. When the wise king suggested cutting the child in two, one of the women immediately cried out and said that she would rather relinquish the child than kill it. Then King Solomon realized that the child belonged to her. It wasn't Lilith, of course.

In various cultures, particularly polytheistic ones, there were figures who partially resembled women, such as the black Indian goddess Kali or the West African witch. The *incubus* and the *succubus*, which were not really vampires, but behaved in a similar manner when they attacked men at night and left them

without their virility and energy in the morning, accompanied Western culture and influenced the developing myth. According to the Greek legend, Menippus, who was one of Apollonius' followers, married a rich woman who became a vampire and systematically sucked all of his vitality from him. Thanks to Apollonius' wisdom, Menippus was saved from death.

In the culture of the Caribbean Islands, it was believed that *Loogaroo* and *Sukuyan* were women who lived "normal" lives during the day among the people of the community, and turned into vampires at night. Even their husbands knew nothing about this.

While each of the above-mentioned mythological figures developed differently in the various cultures, at a certain point in time, they united to form a general picture that characterized the young vampire: a beautiful woman who came from another place with the aim of seducing the innocent male and bringing about his downfall. When the image of the vampire began to be linked more to the death of a beloved person and less to problems of pregnancy and birth, the mythical female vampire was forced to make way for the new vampire.

The figure of the modern vampire is based on two main historical figures: "Vlad the Impaler" (from the 15th century), upon whom Dracula and his successors are based, and Elizabeth Bathory, the Hungarian countess (who lived in the 17th century), and whose blood-curdling story became widely known during the period in which the waves of hysteria about the existence of vampires were at their peak. Countess Bathory was accused of having extracted the blood of her young maidservants and bathing in it in order to keep her skin young and healthy. After torturing and murdering hundreds of women, she was sentenced to life imprisonment. Her story provided Bram Stoker, the author of Dracula, with great inspiration. Stoker was in fact responsible for the creation of the figure of the modern vampire. However, when the vampires reached the pages of literature at the end of the 18th century, here too women got in first. Some of them did not have names, such as Goethe's poem, "The Bride of Corinth", which was published in 1797. Goethe based the poem on the ancient Greek story about a women by the name of Philinnon who died a virgin and returned to life in order to taste the pleasures of sex before leaving the world of the living forever. The writer, Robert Southey, wrote about the protagonist, Thalaba, who succeeded in killing a female vampire that resided in the body of his bride, Oneiza. However, the most important one of all was the vampire Geraldine. At the end of the 1790s, the poet, Samuel Taylor Coleridge, wrote his poem "Christabel" and presented Geraldine, the modern female vampire, to the English readers. This poem tells about the vampire Geraldine who appears in the forest next to an ancient castle one night. The daughter of the owner of the castle, Christabel, notices her and invites her inside. When the two are alone, Geraldine seduces the innocent Christabel and leaves her confused and tired in the morning. Eventually, Geraldine falls into the net of Christabel's father and leaves the castle with him.

After the appearance of Geraldine and her friends, 19th-century vampire literature became filled with almost entirely male vampires, led by Lord Ruthven, the aristocratic vampire originally devised by Lord Byron, and who liked mainly female victims. Polidori's story, which was published in 1819, became successful, and subsequently Lord Ruthven also starred in French plays. He served as the platform for the creation of the British vampire in the first half of that century: *Varney the Vampire.*

In 1836, the short story "Clairmonde" by French writer, Théophile Gautier, was published. It was also called "The Beautiful Vampire". After this, the female vampires found a place for themselves in numerous short stories, from Alexander Dumas' "Pale Lady" (1848) to Sheridan Le Fanu's novella *Carmilla* (1872). The vampire Carmilla also made history when she became the most popular and inspiring female vampire, and she too – just like the other vampires of her time – preferred young women like herself.

For many years, female vampires were limited to short stories only, even though Anne Crawford's story, "A Mystery of the Campagna" (1887) became a classic. Reality changed with the birth of the cinema. In 1936, female vampires began to conquer the big screen with the movie, *Dracula's Daughter*, starring the actress Gloria Holden, who provided a response to the movie, Dracula, in which actor Bela Lugasi played the title role in 1931. Holden portrayed the countess Marya Zaleska, who steals the body of her father and burns it in order to find a way out of her vampiric existence. In the meantime, she does not manage to control her urges and continues seeking victims, until she falls in love with Dr. Jeffrey Garth, former pupil of Dr. Van Helsing, Dracula's killer. When Zaleska realizes that there is no cure for her condition, she leads her lover to Dracula's castle

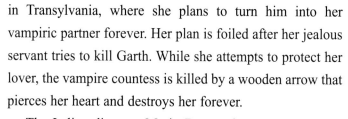

in Transylvania, where she plans to turn him into her vampiric partner forever. Her plan is foiled after her jealous servant tries to kill Garth. While she attempts to protect her lover, the vampire countess is killed by a wooden arrow that pierces her heart and destroys her forever.

The Italian director, Mario Bava, who was responsible for dozens of vampire movies in the 1960s, turned actress Barbara Steele into a popular and threatening vampire among aficionados of the genre. In his movie, *The Mask of Satan* (1960), Steele played Princess Asa, a 17th-century witch who was murdered by a masked man and brought back to life by means of a drop of blood, wreaking terror on the entire community. At the same time, French director Roger Vadim directed his wife, Annette Stroyberg, in the perfect movie role: *Carmilla*. According to Vadim's version, Carmilla attacked her niece Georgia and eventually died after being impaled on a fence post. Another female vampire was portrayed by actress Florence Marly, who starred in Roger Corman's *Queen of Blood*. She is particularly memorable because that movie was one of the first vampire and science fiction movies ever to be screened. The alien Marly, who lived on Mars, viciously attacked the crew of the spaceship that wanted to bring her back to Earth.

The great breakthrough of the female vampires began in the 1970s. Even before their breakthrough into the movies, the writer, Marv Wolfman, created a comic character called Lilith in 1970, and presented her as Dracula's daughter. The successful series of comic books also yielded the movie, *Dracula's Daughter*, in 1992. At the beginning of the decade, several of the best-ever female vampire movies were made. The first was Hammer's movie, *The Vampire Loves*, starring actress Ingrid Pitt, who made a deep impression on the audience. The movie was based both on *Carmilla* and on the story of Elizabeth Bathory. The direction of Roy Ward Baker focused on Carmilla's lesbian episodes with young women, who were attracted over and over again, until Carmilla was caught by a vampire catcher whose daughter had also been attacked by her. The next movie, which was directed by Hammer himself, was called *Lust for a Vampire*, starring Jut Stengard. This time, the movie tells the story of the adventures of the vampire Carmilla in a 19th-century girls' school. Hammer's third movie in the Carmilla trilogy was *Twins of Evil* (1971), starring Katya Wyeth. Here, Carmilla vampirizes her relative, Count Karnstein, and together they struggle with witch-hunter Gustav Weil.

Hammer's trilogy gave broad expression to the raw potential of the vampire, Carmilla, and also served as a source of inspiration for other directors such as Jesus Franco, who directed two Carmilla movies of his own in 1972 and 1973. Although the second movie had a tedious plot, it presented the actress Lina Romay as a modern Carmilla, and was shown many times over under different names – most recently as a video entitled *Erotikill*. In 1974, another Carmilla movie reached the screen. In it, she seduces a frigid bride. The abandoned bridegroom finds his bride sleeping with the female vampire in their coffin.

The story of Elizabeth Bathory also served as a source of inspiration for many creators. Hammer directed Countess

Dracula starring Ingrid Pitt, a movie that became famous mainly because of Pitt's nude scenes. At the same time, the Belgian movie, *Daughters of Darkness*, was released. Here, Bathory befriends a young couple, and after the husband reveals himself to be a sadist, his wife and Bathory decide to kill him. Later, Bathory is murdered and the wife (who has meanwhile become a vampire) replaces her.

Thus, despite the dominance of the famous Dracula, several female vampires found their way to the screen thanks to the movies that were based on the characters of Carmilla and Elizabeth Bathory – mainly in the 1970s.

During the next decade, several female vampires became justifiably renowned. The first was Mariam Blaylock, the foreign vampire from the movie, *The Hunger*, played by French actress Catherine Deneuve. The story focused on Blaylock's eternal problem: the men she loves age too quickly and die. In her desire to rescue her current lover (actor David Bowie), she seduces a blood researcher (Susan Sarandon) who, despite her attempts, ultimately fails to find a cure for the lover's aging problem. In contrast to this dramatic situation, the movie *Once Bitten* (1985) was a comedy, in which Lauren Hutton plays a vampire who is searching for the blood of a virgin in modern-day Hollywood. Eventually she attacks actor Jim Carrey, and his girlfriend is forced to sacrifice her virginity in order to save him from death.

EMBASSY HOME ENTERTAINMENT®

The Velvet Vampire

She's waiting to love you... to death.

In 1986, the movie *The Vamp* was screened, starring singer Grace Jones, who was very impressive with her unique appearance. Jones plays the manageress of a nightclub in the movie. One night, a group of students comes to her in their quest for a stripper for a party. One of the boys accompanies Jones home, and she "vampirizes" him. Even though the movie suffered from a problem of identity (was it a comedy or a horror movie?), the uniqueness with which Jones endowed the vampire character left an unforgettable impression on the audience.

Other less prominent female vampires of the 1980s were played by actresses Gabrielle Lazure, Matilda May, Britt Ekland, Sylvia Kristel, and Julie Carmen. Other women, such as Katt Shea Ruben, made their mark as directors. Ruben did not create the image of a female vampire, but rather that of a victim – a strong and clever woman, who, after describing the nature of daylight to the gloomy vampire, managed to stave off his attack as dawn broke. Another director is Kathryn Bigelow, who directed the movie *Near Dark*, about a modern vampire band that roamed the countryside in a large van. A guy joins the band, and he is attracted to one of the female members, actress Jenny Wright. After he becomes a vampire, he is unable to kill and suck the blood of his innocent victims, and is forced to rely on Wright for his sustenance.

In 1992, an impressive vampire movie starring actress Anne Parilland became famous: *Innocent Blood*. Parilland played a cautious modern

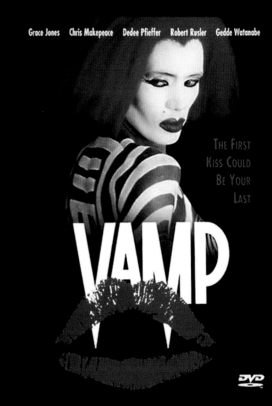

Grace Jones   Chris Makepeace   Dedee Pfieffer   Robert Rusler   Gedde Watanabe

THE FIRST KISS COULD BE YOUR LAST

VAMP

DVD

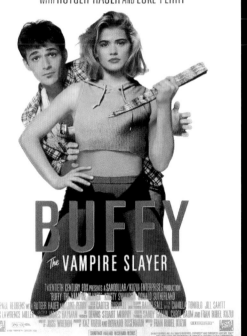

vampire who has learned to survive by means of certain rules according to which she lives, such as not playing with her food, and cleaning up properly after her meals. One evening, when she does not manage to finish her dinner – which consists of an overgrown Mafioso – the guy rises up in the middle of her sucking his blood and becomes a vampire himself. In order to restrain the new and bloodthirsty vampire, the female vampire is compelled to seek the succor of a human police officer.

That same year, the movie *Buffy the Vampire Slayer* was screened, breaking new records. This time, the protagonist was a young, athletic girl, a high-school cheerleader, who was chosen to kill the King of the Undead and the rest of the vampires with him. A series developed from the movie, and it scored extremely high ratings and huge success.

Modern literature today boasts several famous female vampire authors such as Elaine Bergstrom, P. N. Elrod and Anne Rice, but they have opted for male vampire protagonists in their novels. The female vampires that have penetrated the literature of the 20th century mainly starred in short stories. However, the most important female vampire appeared that same

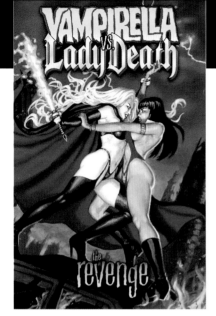

year not in a novel, but in the *Vampirella* comic books. These dazzlingly successful comic books featured a mischievous and sexy female vampire from the planet Drakulon. The series was compiled by Ron Goulart in six volumes in the mid-1970s, and recently the lovable comic character has come back to life and gained renewed popularity.

The figure of the female vampire that was created was quite different than that of the power-hungry male vampire. It depicted female powers in its personality, too. The male vampires also became more complex in modern literature than they had been in previous centuries. The vampire character at the beginning of the century, which represented male lusts for power and sex, left the female character with little else to do than serve as a stereotypical victim. However, as we have mentioned, over the decades, the male vampire characters became even more colorful, and the women they confronted were given roles other than that of the victim.

Vampires and sexuality

*I*n order to comprehend the power and influence of the vampire, we must examine his sexual nature, among other things. When scholars began to investigate the phenomenon – both in literature and in folklore – they noticed sexual themes that emerged from the testimonies and the stories.

In the folklore from the southern Slavic countries, especially among the Gypsies, it was believed that the vampire was a sexual being, and that what motivated him and caused him to rise from his grave was in fact his highly developed sex drive. According to the Gypsy belief, the first thing a vampire does upon rising from the grave is to return to his widow. Each night he comes to her in order to have sexual intercourse with her, and leaves her totally exhausted in the morning. In many cases, the widows would become pregnant by their dead husbands, and the resulting child was called a *dhampir* and was thought to have the ability to identify and eliminate vampires. Another popular theme among the Gypsies stated that the vampire would return to the woman with whom he had been in love during his life, but had never been able to consummate his love for her. He invites his beloved to his grave, where he makes love with her and makes her "his" for all eternity.

In Russia, too, vampires were described as sexual creatures. It was customary to tell about the young, handsome man who appeared in the village and wandered around among the youngsters, seducing young women. Of course, he was a vampire. In Malaysia, the *langsuyar* was the star. She was the sexual vampire that lived in the village for years as a young married woman with children, without anyone becoming aware of what she got up to as a vampire at night.

In Bram Stoker's famous novel, *Dracula*, the hidden sexual stratum can be discerned, even though it is concealed from the readers' consciousness and perhaps from the author's consciousness as well. Modern literature from the 19th century features many stories about vampires, expressing their sexuality far more openly than the famous vampire, Dracula. However, pornographic movies that featured vampire protagonists were extremely rare.

Movies and novels were responsible for the change in the image of the vampire – from the traditional monster image of previous generations to the romantic and seductive lover of today. Since the end of the 19th century, the American vampire has become more humorous and sexy than terrifying and monstrous. Most of the vampires from the last decades of the 20th century make sure to include elements of both terror and sexuality in their personalities. For many people, the vampire has become a symbol of powerful energies and emotionality as a result of his sexual and impulse-driven behavior. In this way, no doubt, the vampire has adapted himself to the expectations of the readers and viewers, as well as to the expectations of the entire culture.

Homosexual and lesbian vampires

Lesbian relations between the female vampire and her victim were the first to appear in the traditional vampire literature of the 18th century. This trend extended into the 19th century as well, and has recently come to the fore in the cinema. It seems that the sexual nature of the vampires and the complex relations between them and their victims were expressed in homosexuality and lesbianism for many creators, who used vampires to interpret these relations in various ways.

As we have mentioned, the first vampires were actually women (the *langsuyer* in Malaysia, the *lamiai* in Greece), and the first historical acknowledgement of vampires in the Western world involved Elizabeth Bathory, "the countess of blood", who lived in the 17th century and was related to the Hungarian royal family. Bathory was accused of the murder of hundreds of young girls and of drinking their blood. The few that survived her tortures testified that the countess bathed in her victims' blood in order to preserve her youth. All of her victims were young women. Of Anna Darvulia, her personal assistant in the ghastly crimes, it was said that she was a lesbian who liked wearing suits and trousers and playing men's games.

It seems that under the influence of the story of Bathory, it was preferable to describe the vampire in literature as a woman with high social status who seduced or attacked young, classless women, usually students or servants. And just as the male vampires favored their victims in the form of young and beautiful women, so did the female vampires. When the relations between a vampire and his victim became sexual, the attitude of the female vampires toward their female victims also became sexual. This was usually expressed in forcible sex and rape.

The first vampire poem, "Christabel", was published in 1816. It was written by Samuel Taylor Coleridge, who was the first to present the theme that would later recur over and over again in vampire literature: lesbian relations between female vampires and their victims. The poem tells about the vampire Geraldine who appears in a forest next to the castle of young

Christabel's father. Christabel sees Geraldine and invites her to the castle. The two drink wine together and become intoxicated. Geraldine suggests that Christabel undress. The latter does as she is told, and gets into bed. Geraldine joins her. What goes on between the sheets is hinted at rather than stated explicitly. In the morning, Geraldine wakes up fresh, while Christabel gets out of bed confused and guilt-ridden, and immediately goes out to pray. In spite of everything, Christabel chooses to introduce Geraldine to her father. Unfortunately, Geraldine finds a way to pull the wool over the eyes of the naive Sir Leoline, who abandons his daughter and the castle and goes off with the vampire Geraldine.

The lesbian relations between the vampire Geraldine and the young Christabel were a source of great inspiration for Sheridan Le Fanu's short story, "Carmilla", which was written in 1872. Some people considered it to be a kind of prose rewrite of "Christabel". Carmilla, too, is invited to a catle, this time by unsuspecting guests who notice her standing outside. She seduces 19-year-old Laura, also the daughter of the owner of the castle. Le Fanu chose to highlight the sexual element even more, and he describes how Carmilla embraces Laura, kisses her neck, holds her close to her cheek and kisses her. Laura tries to resist Carmilla, but finds herself devoid of strength. Eventually, Carmilla dies before killing Laura, but she does manage to kill the neighbor's daughter.

In 1936, the movie *Dracula's Daughter* came out. It told the story of the countess Zaleska, who satisfied her lust for the blood of several gorgeous models. Twenty years later, the movie, *Blood of Dracula*, told the story of a teenage female vampire who attacks her classmates. In 1971, the movie *Daughters of Darkness*, which was inspired by the story of Elizabeth Bathory, was screened. In the 1960s and 1970s, several movies inspired by the story "Carmilla" were screened. They were considered lesbian movies, even though they actually portrayed beautiful women who fulfilled the male fantasy about lesbian relations. Among them was *Blood and Roses* (1960), *Vampire Lovers* (1970), *Lust for a Vampire* (1971) and *Twins of Evil* (1971). In 1974, the movie *Vampyres* came out, describing the murder of a lesbian couple by a homophobic man. The two lesbians

return from the dead as a pair of vampires and together they attack successive male victims. Lesbian scenes were also featured in movies such as *The Hunger* (1986), starring Catherine Deneuve and Susan Sarandon, *Mark of Lilith* (1986), and *Because the Dawn* (1988). These movies presented the lesbian vampires in a more credible light than simply as a response to a male fantasy. Lesbian vampire literature was produced by authors for lesbian readers during the last decade of the 20th century. It presented – albeit in a slightly delusional manner – lesbian relations that were closer to reality than to the male fantasy.

It is difficult to say that homosexual vampires are very common. The male vampires of the 19th century apparently preferred the blood of young women. At the same time, there is no mention of vampires who preferred to attack men, and if they did do that, it happened under the influence of drugs or medications.

In literature there were very few gay vampires. The writer, Jeffrey McMahan, published several short stories, some of which featured gay vampire protagonists. He invented Andrew, the gay vampire, who later became the protagonist of the novel, *Vampires Anonymous*. The novel describes a modern vampire hunt by a group of people who were attacked in the past. However, the modern author, Anne Rice, actually chose to write about gay vampires. In her book, *Interview with the Vampire*, the complex and tense relations between Louis and Lestat the vampire are described, and there are sexual connotations that did not escape the critics' eyes. Rice raised gender issues, not necessarily connected to sex, and created the androgynous aspect of the vampire. Lestat the vampire was generally involved in close ties with men and was described as someone who cried frequently. However, when he exchanged his body for that of someone else, he had to rape a woman. As in most of Rice's books, a vampire cannot have "normal" sexual relations, and instead, Rice suggested that the act of sucking blood and biting provided even greater pleasure than the sexual act and served as a substitute for it. And indeed, the reciprocal bloodsucking in which Lestat and Louis indulge is analogous to having full intercourse, according to Rice. Rice's books – which served as a source for the modern Gothic rock movement that espoused androgyny – were full of various sexual expressions, including homosexual, sadomasochistic and transvestite ones.

The gods pondered what to do with the work, one of them has the idea of creating a race of slaves who would produce cultures, images, offerings and sacrifices. In this way was created the human race.

Mesopotamic legend, 2500 B.C.

"Real" vampires

According to the dictionary, the vampire is a kind of small bat found mainly in South America. One of its properties is that of sucking the blood of its prey while the latter is sleeping. The prey can be bovine or human – and this is the origin of the nomenclature "vampire" for the legendary creature that is in the habit of attacking human beings in their sleep. The term "vampire" has also been borrowed to describe a person who exploits other people's strength ruthlessly.

However, it seems that there are three types of vampire-bats. They are found in Mexico, Central America and South America. They were discovered in the 16th century by European biologists, who identified them as vampires. As we said before, because of its properties, it was called a "vampire" and became an integral part of the modern vampire myth of our time.

Bats are the only mammals that can fly. There are almost one thousand types of bats, and they spend most of their time asleep, hanging upside-down. From this position, they plunge to the ground, rise up into the air and fly. The most common vampire-bat is the Desmodus rotundus, while the rarer ones are the Diasemus youngi and the Diphylla ecandota. These are different than the rest of the bats in their feeding habits. While bats feed on fruit and plants and/or various insects, vampire-bats feed mainly on the blood of animals. The Diasemus and the Diphylla prefer bird blood, while the Desmodus – the best-known – feeds mainly on the blood of other mammals.

Desmodus rotundus

Bats' teeth resemble sharp scissors, which they use to cut into the living flesh. Unlike the mythical hero, bats actually let the blood flow and lap it up with their tongues, like a cat lapping milk. Bats are mobile and quick, and they can walk, run and jump. Their sense of smell is highly developed and their big eyes enable them to see clearly over a broad expanse. An average-size adult vampire-bat consumes about 15 milliliters of blood per night – about 40 percent of its body weight. After the meal, its stomach looks distended, and he needs a long time in order to digest properly.

The vampire-bat constituted a serious problem for the peasants of South America, since their cattle served as excellent food for the bat. Their repeated attempts to catch it failed. Over the years, many legends sprang up in South American folklore regarding these lethal vampire-bats, such as the one that was common among the ancient Mayans of Guatemala regarding the vampire Camazotz. It was said that he sprang up and rose from the underworld.

Vampire-bats also appeared in the folklore of Western culture, even though up to the 19th century, they were not associated with the myth, just as there was no connection between the "vampire" and the image of the bat. Over the years – apparently because vampires live at night – the bats, just like owls, were associated with the creatures of the unknown and supernatural world. In Greek mythology, on which Western folklore is based, bats were sacred animals for Proserpine, the wife of Pluto, god of the underworld. By definition, bats became synonymous with Satan and evil, and from here it was just a short distance to death.

Cultures in which the bats have positive associations must be mentioned. Among the Gypsies, for instance, they always symbolized good luck. The gypsies would prepare small purses from dried bats' organs and would place them around children's necks as an amulet. In Macedonia, too, bats' bones symbolized good luck.

In the Spanish culture, bloodsucking bats became more human vampires. Their description focused more on fact that they were bloodsuckers than on their other properties. It was the beginning of the connection between the bat and the vampire, which would later be expressed and have a place in the modern Western world. In his epic, "Jerusalem", William Blake used the bat to symbolize the psychological and pathological part of the human brain. In the works of Francisco Goya, bats appeared as a similar symbol.

Only in 1897, with the publication of the novel *Dracula*, was the identity of the vampire-bat formed. In Bram Stoker's book, the bat appeared as one of the nocturnal creatures controlled by Dracula. At the beginning of the story, Dracula appeared as a bat; he turned into a bat when he flew out of the window of the room in which Jonathan Harker was staying in his castle. When Dracula moves to England, he is present more as a bat than in human form, and always appears at night.

More about the world of the vampire

*T*he image of the vampire includes, among other things, the special fangs that became its dominant symbol. In his book, *Dracula*, Bram Stoker wrote that the vampire's mouth looked cruel because of his sharp white teeth, which extended over his lip. When he smiled, the vampire's teeth were exposed and appeared even more threatening. The vampire's three wives are also described as having similar teeth. These teeth are used when Dracula attacks his victim, Lucy Westenra. After her death, it looks as if they too are becoming longer and sharper. However, Dracula was not the first to possess such fangs. "Varney the Vampire" is also described as having sharp teeth, which he plunged into the neck of his victim, Flora, before sucking her blood. The vampire's fangs serve as a focal point. When people notice them, they immediately know that they are looking at a vampire. It would seem that the vampire's fangs are the last thing that remains of the folkloristic figure.

Dracula's fingernails in Stoker's book are also described as long and pointed. These nails reflect the animal aspects that exist in Dracula the vampire. Later on in the story, Stoker describes how Dracula uses them effectively when he scratches and wounds the chest of his victim in order to drink his blood. According to the reports that circulated in eastern Europe, Germany and the Slavic countries, vampire hunters described, among other things, how the fingernails of the deceased continued to grow in his grave after his death, and that fresh new fingernails replaced the dead ones. These descriptions might have formed the basis for the description of the image of today's vampire. While the long, curved fingernails of the vampire count were prominent in the movie *Nosferatu* (1922), it was deemed preferable to ignore this aspect in the movie *Dracula* (1931), when actor Bela Lugosi appeared with neatly clipped fingernails.

When describing the world of the vampire, it is impossible to ignore several significant aspects that exist in it. One of the popular notions states that the vampire's reflection is not visible in a mirror, and this notion was expressed in Western culture for the first time in the Stoker's novel, *Dracula*. There it is told that when Jonathan Harker arrives at Dracula's castle, he notices that there are no mirrors in the building. While he is shaving, Dracula enters his room and stands behind him. Then Harker notices that Dracula's reflection is not visible in the mirror. Stoker did not make up this idea himself. In the Eastern European culture, it was thought for generations that mirrors had the power to revive the spirit of the deceased. This is because they believed that while the person was still alive, his soul was reflected in the reflection in the mirror. When a person sees himself in the mirror, he believes in his own existence and in the existence of his soul, and this is a kind of testimony to the fact that life goes on. However, there were people who considered the reflection to be a reason for fear, since the mirror was liable to exert a negative influence on the soul. This is also the source of the superstition that a broken mirror is a sign of seven years' bad luck in a house, and that breaking a mirror signifies potential damage to the soul.

However, as we know, vampires do not have souls. This is the reason that their reflection is not visible in the mirror. The mirror, therefore, confronts the vampire with his eternal existence – that he is neither alive nor dead.

Another motif that characterizes the world of the vampires is mist. The idea that a vampire can turn into mist was of minor importance in Western folklore. Nevertheless, this possibility could answer the question of how vampires were able to get in and out of their graves without moving the soil that covers the coffin – a question that was asked after small holes in the ground were found in the vicinity of the grave. In Bram Stoker's *Dracula*, Dracula transforms himself into mist when he sails on a ship to England. In this way, he can get out of the dark box in which he was resting, and get back sinto it undisturbed. This is also how he can go through closed doors.

In Eastern European folklore, it was believed that vampires rest in their graves in the local cemetery during the day, and get up to stalk their victims at night. They can rest when they are surrounded by "native soil". In the early vampire literature,

this soil was not mentioned, and it appears for the first time in Bram Stoker's book. It turns out that Dracula the vampire prefers to lie in a box full of his grave soil and in his native soil, with additional boxes containing exactly the same soil placed next to him. Dr. Van Helsing, the vampire catcher, discovers Dracula's secret. He realizes that the vampire needs his native soil while he is resting there, and if this soil is destroyed, it will also destroy Dracula. Helsing succeeds in destroying all of the boxes but one, in which Dracula manages to hide and flee to Transylvania, where he subsequently dies. Over the years, other creators developed the idea that the vampire draws his strength from the native soil.

The inseparable link between vampires and coffins is rooted in the simple fact that vampires were once dead people, and dead people are generally buried in coffins. However, vampires existed even before people began to be buried in coffins. Until recent centuries, coffins were the preserve of people who could afford them. The rest of the deceased were wrapped in fabric and buried directly in the ground. During the times when the plague raged throughout Europe, it was customary to bury the dead speedily. As a result, the graves were not deep enough and were liable to be ravaged by various predators. In order to prevent animals from digging up the grave of the deceased, it was customary to place a flat rock on the mouth of the shallow grave.

At the beginning of the 18th century, more people were buried in coffins, except that by then, the vampire plague was inspiring terror in the hearts of many people. In order to avoid the return of the deceased to life, the coffin would be left open, and the corpse would be nailed to it. In certain places, it sufficed to nail the dead person's clothing to the sides of the coffin, and only then could it be lowered into the grave. Perhaps the reason for the fact that it is customary to kill the vampire by driving a wooden stake into his body stems from the ancient custom of nailing the corpse to the coffin. If this hypothesis is true, it means that the stake need not be driven through the vampire's heart, because for purposes of nailing the corpse in place, the back or abdomen is satisfactory. The fact that stakes made of various types of wood or iron were used reinforces this hypothesis.

According to the folkloristic tradition, vampires sleep in their coffins. When they move from place to place, they take their coffins with them. Having said that, the early literary vampires did not have coffins, and even in Bram Stoker's *Dracula*, Dracula did not move around in his coffin, but rather needed it in order to safeguard his native soil. When the

vampire hunter, Dr. Van Helsing, arrives at Dracula's castle in order to kill him, he finds several coffins there, one of which is engraved with the immortal name: **Dracula**.

In 1931, when the movie *Dracula*, based on the novel of the same name, was screened for the first time, it began by showing the vampires rising out of their coffins in the basement of the castle and going outside. In later movies, the coffin was exchanged for boxes containing Dracula's native soil, which he conveyed with him to England. However, many movies featured vampires waking up in their coffins and getting out of them in order to carry out their schemes. In more modern movies, the coffin is mainly used for storing the vampire's native soil. Nevertheless, we must remember that in the 20th century, the vampire lost touch with his native soil, and the role of the coffin was reduced to the fact of its being the vampire's refuge against daylight. Not only did the coffin serve to create a certain atmosphere in the movie, but it was responsible for creating comic moments that involved moving it from place to place, protecting it, and many weird and wonderful explanations for its appearance. The coffin also served as a convenient target for the vampire hunter, since it was easier to catch the vampire in it during the day.

Author Anne Rice, who bears more than a little responsibility for the development of the myth of the modern vampire, opted to ascribe particular importance to the coffin in her novels. In her well-known book, *Interview with the Vampire*, Lestat the vampire sleeps in a coffin, and on the night he transforms Louis into a vampire, he forgets to get hold of a coffin for him. When dawn comes, the two have no choice but to hide together from the daylight in Lestat's coffin. However, Rice's vampires could simply have returned to the earth (as the vampire Lestat had done for many years), or, alternatively, they could have remained shut up in the cell that protected them from the sunlight. Thus, even though there is no urgent necessity for coffins, most vampires prefer to sleep in them. Only after coffins had existed for many years was it understood that all vampires needed was protection against the daylight, and that was the purpose of the coffins and their substitutes – just like Dracula's boxes.

It is common knowledge that the best-known and most effective way to kill a vampire is by driving a wooden stake through his heart. This method is described well in Sheridan Le Fanu's story, "Carmilla", and afterwards in Bram Stoker's novel, *Dracula*. This process was recreated very faithfully in the later vampire movies. The idea originated from the nailing of the dead body to the coffin or to the ground in order to prevent it from rising up from its grave, climbing out of it, and coming back to life as a vampire. This ancient method was prevalent throughout Europe, and it was mainly used with dead people who ran a high risk of becoming vampires (that is, those who had died unusual deaths or had committed suicide, for instance). In this way, it was ensured that the deceased would remain in his optimal place: in a grave and in the world of the dead. The easiest way to impale a vampire was either through his stomach, or, when he was lying on his stomach, through his back. In most places, it was preferable to impale vampires with wooden stakes, but in some places, an iron stake or even a long needle was used – anything that could prevent the deceased from rising up from his grave. When coffins began to be used, the purpose of the stake changed slightly. The prevailing idea at the time stated that only by attacking the vampire's heart – which pumps the blood – was it possible to eliminate him entirely. In Russian literature, there are good descriptions of how the stake must be driven into the body in one fateful stab, since any subsequent stab was liable to bring the vampire back to life. A

great deal has been written about stakes made of wood, mainly because of the belief that wood has the power to deter the vampire (this is because Jesus' cross was made of wood). Ultimately, the function of the stake was to harm the heart physically: to be driven into it and to remain stuck there. If it came out, the deceased would come to life and would embark on his dangerous vampire existence.

The prevailing belief stated that garlic had even greater power to deter vampires than the holy cross. This is the reason why, for generations and in many cultures, garlic was used against vampires on a daily basis, since all vampires are revolted by it. In his book, *Dracula*, Bram Stoker describes how Dr. Van Helsinger uses garlic when he arrives in order to treat the young Lucy Westenra, who was attacked by the vampire. Dr. Van Helsinger holds a box containing cloves of garlic, and he hangs them around Lucy's neck in order to keep the vampire away from her.

Garlic is a vital element. After the vampire was killed by having a stake driven through his heart, and sometimes by being beheaded just to make sure, it was customary to stuff cloves of garlic into his mouth.

However, it must be remembered that this treatment is only effective for the vampires that have emerged in recent generations, since the older ones among them can turn into mist or dust the moment the wooden stake is driven through them. Garlic was also used as a remedy for other ailments. During the 12th century, and mainly in the Slavic countries, it was believed that garlic had remedial powers against other forces of evil, such as witches and other satanic entities. In the countries that were close to Romania, garlic was closely linked to the vampire myth.

Garlic also occurred in the tradition of Mexico and the South American countries, and even in China. Over the generations, with the disappearance of the cross as a deterrent against vampires, good old garlic remained as a safe and effective weapon.

European folklore also reports the use of various grains and seeds as a means of protection against vampires. The type of seeds changed from place to place, the most commonly used being mustard seeds, which are mentioned in the New Testament. Millet seeds were also popular, as were flax seeds, carrot seeds, and rice. The reason for sprinkling seeds in the coffin was to amuse the vampire, but it was even more customary to sprinkle them on the grave and next to it, as well as along the path that led from the cemetery to the village or to the home of the deceased. The aim was to capture the attention of the vampire. So long as he was busy gathering the seeds or counting them, there was a chance that his return to the village would be delayed that night, and he would not attack the inhabitants. The more seeds they spread, the longer the vampire's sojourn in the world of the dead would be, and the longer his return to the living would be delayed.

Another thing vampires despise is sunlight. However, this was not always the case. In many cultures, vampires were able to return to human life and infiltrate human society. In 19th-century literature, vampires wandered around freely during the day, as, for instance, in the early vampire poem by Samuel Taylor Coleridge, "Christabel", and in other poems. It seems that the modern vampire resumed functioning as a nocturnal creature in the movie, *Nosferatu*, in 1922, followed by the movie *Dracula* and other movies. Sunlight became a deadly factor for the vampire, and its main role was to limit him. It obstructed the vampire's capabilities, and this served to create a boundary for his activities and movement. The sunrise and the sunset create the time boundaries for the vampire's activity, and the rising dawn could create a dramatic effect of tension in the plot – in literature and particularly in movies.

The literary vampire had another problem: water. According to Dr. Van Helsinger, the vampire hunter from the novel *Dracula*, a vampire can pass through running water only if it is very shallow. However, this trait was unique only to Dracula himself. Having said that, the vampire St. Germain, the protagonist of author Yarbro's novel, had a problem crossing water. He only succeeded in doing so by means of the native soil he carried in the hollow heels of his shoes, and from which he drew his strength. The traditional folkloristic vampires also had problems with water. In Russia, for example, it was customary to throw the body of a suspected vampire into the river, because the earth would not tolerate his existence. In Germany, too, it was customary to throw the body of a person who had committed suicide into the river. In other parts of the country, water would be poured over the grave as well as along the path leading to the home of the deceased. This was done in order to prevent his return to his former place of residence. In Prussia, water was used to wash off the body in the hopes that in this way it might be rescued from the fate of becoming a vampire. Water has purifying powers and plays a part in various mythical and religious rituals. The Baptists baptize the infant as a symbol of his belonging to the religion. The Jews and the Moslems dip themselves in water in order to purify themselves before praying. In Christianity, too, the holy water symbolizes the values of cleanliness and integrity, and is used in religious rituals. It should be mentioned that the use of water against vampires was prevalent mainly in the novels and movies of the 20th century – far more than in the previous century.

However, over and above everything, it turns out that fire is the ultimate and most effective weapon against vampires. Fire is the only thing that can destroy them totally – at least that is what was believed in Eastern European countries. Fire serves as an ancient symbol of the presence of God, as is evidenced by the Bible story of the burning bush and the story of the destruction of Sodom and Gomorrah. The ancient writings relate to fire as an element of destruction, but also as an element of renewal. It destroys the old and the corrupt, and makes room for the new and the pure. Throughout the world, fire was always an essential source of light and heat. A spark of vitality is described as a source of fire. In certain countries, fire was used to purify the earth of elements that were harmful to human society, as reflected, for instance, in the burning of witches in the Middle Ages. When the vampire attacked the herds of cattle, the villagers would light bonfires at equal distances from one another around the herd, in the hopes that they would trap the vampire. In Bulgaria, Romania, Russia and Poland, it was believed that if the vampire were not killed by the wooden stake or by being beheaded, fire would come along and finish him off.

Vampires in Japan

The various mythical creatures in Japanese folklore did not include the classic bloodsuckers that we know as vampires. Of all the mythological beings, the one that most resembles the vampire as we know it seems to be the kappa. The *kappa* entered the Japanese culture in a massive way, and to this day they feature in Japanese literature, art and leisure activities. According to texts from the 18th century, the kappa are described as water creatures that lived in rivers, ponds, lakes and seas, and actually looked like human children with greenish-yellow skin and webbed hands and feet, like the other water creatures. They somewhat resembled monkeys with long noses and round eyes, and had a shell like a turtle that smelled like fish. The kappa's strength was contingent on the amount of water contained by their concave heads, and if it spilled, the kappa lost their strength.

The kappa operated from the banks of the lake and from the edge of the pond. They could be seen mainly in the rural areas. According to the many stories about them, the kappa would ambush horses and cows at the side of the road and near water, catch them and drag them into the water, where they would suck their blood. The act of sucking blood constitutes the kappa's only similarity to the Western vampire. However, it is also known that the kappa would get out of the water to steal melons and cucumbers and to attack people and extract their livers. In order to protect themselves against the kappa, or, more precisely, in order to placate them, the Japanese would write their own names and the names of the members of their families on a cucumber and throw it into the river where they believed the dangerous kappa lived. Nothing has been written about people who attacked the kappa, but we do know about various relationships that occurred between humans and kappa.

Another interesting Japanese folktale concerned "the vampire cat of Nabeshima". It told of the prince of Nabeshima and his lovely concubine, Otoyo. One night, a large vampire cat broke into Otoyo's room and killed her. The cat took on Otoyo's appearance, and in this guise came to the prince every night and sapped his vitality. This occurred while the prince's guards mysteriously fell asleep on the job. One day, one of the young guards managed to stay awake, and he noticed the vampire cat in the guise of the girl. He stood in front of it and denied it access to the prince for a few nights. During this time, the prince recovered, and gradually realized that the "girl" was actually an evil spirit that had returned to attack him. The young guard, along with other guards, raced to the girl's apartment. The vampire cat managed to escape to the mountains,

and soon reports of its evil deeds began to arrive. With the help of a large team of people, the prince went to capture the cat, and eventually succeeded in killing it. This folktale was turned into a play by the name of "Vampire Cat" that was staged in 1918. It was also adapted for the screen in 1969.

The last generation in Japan espoused the myth of the European vampire, contributing a bit of its own to it as well. This can be seen mainly in the movie industry. The modern Japanese vampire is called a *kyuketsuki*, and it was created in 1956 in the movie of the same name. The plot of the movie contains several murders, in which all of the victims were found with teeth marks on their necks. However, in the end, it turned out that the murderer was not the vampire. Three years later, the same director made another movie, which told the story of a real vampire that abducted the wife of a renowned atomic scientist. In the 1970s, additional vampire movies were made in Japan, inspired by the Western director, Hammer, and the movie *Dracula* was screened for the first time in Japan in 1979. A year later, an animated vampire movie with mischievous characters appeared, and in 1984, the Japanese version of the story of Elizabeth Bathory became famous.

Vampires in India

Among all the supernatural creatures in the world of Indian belief and religion, there are some that had vampire characteristics and have been mentioned in the vampire literature. The Indian vampires and their cronies occurred for the first time in the ancient Indian texts.

According to Hinduism – the dominant religion in India – the creation started off as a golden egg that contained the entire cosmic intelligence. The creation that we can see is the division of the egg into the heavens, the earth, and the 21 regions of the cosmos. Each of these regions was subdivided into three areas, and each of these was called a *tala*, and consisted of ogres, specters and demons.

Vampires exist in the form of *rakshasas*, which are usually described as demons that live in cemeteries and bother human beings during their various religious rituals. The rakshasas appear in various forms, as men or women, with human characteristics or animal characteristics. The shape of the human-type rakshasas is reminiscent of the monkeys. They are described in the Indian epic, and many mythical heroes are renowned for the fact that they slew one or two rakshasas during their lives.

The rakshasas' resemblance to vampires is rooted in several shared traits. Like the vampires, they too are creatures that wander around at night and have a terrifying appearance that includes long, sharp fangs. In the texts, they are described as bloodthirsty, and seek mainly female victims –

preferably pregnant ones. Moreover, the rakshasas were known to attack infants. The natural enemy of the rakshasas was Agni, who helped human beings eliminate rakshasas.

Another vampire-like creature that exists in India is the *yatu-dhana*, and it is mentioned in the texts alongside the rakshasas. Other creatures, called pisachas, had an even less human appearance. The literal meaning of the name is "eaters of raw flesh", and this creature is described as particularly bloodthirsty. The *bhuta* are the souls of the dead, especially of those who died an untimely death, or of insane, brain-damaged or deformed people. These souls wandered around at night and appeared as dark shadows. Sometimes they tried to return to their bodies. The bhuta would walk around cremation grounds (in India, it is customary to cremate corpses rather than to bury them) and deserts. The bhuta – the evil and dangerous spirits – would eat filthy food and were always thirsty. Their particular love of milk spurred them on to attack infants that had just been fed. The bhuta could transform themselves into other night creatures, such as owls and bats. It should be mentioned that owls have a special status in Indian mythology, and the Indians believe that when the hooting of the owl is heard, it is a sign of bad luck. The Indians use the flesh of the owl in religious rituals and various spells.

Other creatures that are more similar to the Western vampire are the betails or vetales that, like the bhuta, are also ghosts. The betails feature in the classic story from Indian literature, *The Vetala-Pachisi*, which was translated into English by Sir Richard Burton in 1870 and published under the title *Vikram and the Vampire*. It tells the story of King Vikram, who, just like King Arthur in English literature, was also a realistic figure from the first century AD and served as a source of inspiration for many stories. A certain yogi came to King Vikram and enticed him into spending a night with him in the cemetery. There, he persuaded the king to bring him a body from another burial ground that lay at some distance from where they were. Vikram set out and found the body hanging on a mimosa tree, and it turned out that it was a betail. Although it was very difficult for Vikram to bring the betail back with him, he returned to the yogi. He then noticed that the latter was invoking the goddess Kali, because he was surrounded by ghouls and demons, among them rakshasas and bhuta, who had assumed animal forms. The yogi led them to Kali's shrine. When the yogi was about to kill the king, the latter got in first and eliminated him, thus saving Kali. In return for that, the gods granted King Vikram fame.

Many of the Indian demons deceived people by assuming human forms. Before attacking their victims, they discarded these forms and appeared as frightening and threatening creatures once more. One of them was the *churel*, a woman who had died an unnatural death. If she had suffered at the hands of her family during her lifetime, she would return to haunt them and suck their blood. If she succeeded in tempting a young man to partake of the food she had prepared for him, she was liable to keep him with her until dawn and then send him back to his village as an old man. She could be identified by her feet, which were back to front, her toes facing backward and her heels facing forward.

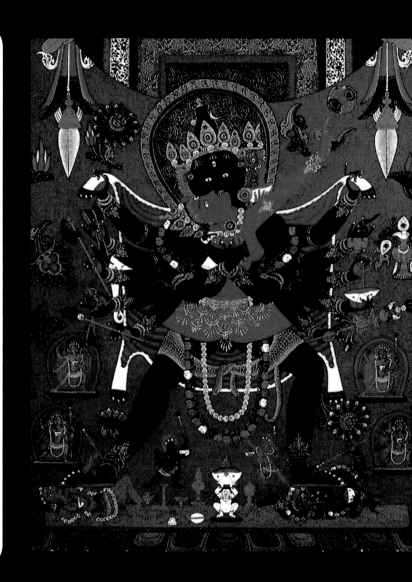

Another belief that prevailed in India stated that a woman who died in childbirth was liable to become a ghost. In order to prevent this, the family deviated from the custom of burning her body, and buried her instead. After the burial, the family drove four nails into the corners of the grave soil and planted red flowers on the grave. The grave was located in a special place, and prior to the burial, the body was taken out of the house through a side door, so as to prevent it from finding its way back into the house. It was buried at noon, in the shade. Here too it was customary to sprinkle seeds on the path between the house and the grave, just like in Eastern Europe, so that the spirit of the woman would busy itself counting them, and this occupation would prevent her from coming back to life.

There were also female vampires called *chedipe* (which literally means "prostitute"). Chedipe were women who would enter the home of a sleeping man naked, suck his blood from his toes, and keep the rest of the members of the household in a hypnotic state so that they would not notice what was going on. In the morning, the man would wake up devoid of energy, as if drunk. If he was not taken care of immediately, the chedipe was liable to return. Moreover, the chedipe would attack people in the jungle by transforming herself into a tiger with human feet.

The researcher Devendra P. Varma claimed that the ancient Hindu vampires constituted the source of the beliefs in vampires in the West. He claimed that these beliefs were brought to the West by the Arabs who migrated along the Silk Route from the Indus Valley into the Mediterranean Basin. They probably reached Greece in approximately the first century AD and spread the myth there. From there, it spread to the West. This theory is certainly possible. In many different cultures, the vampire myth met everybody's basic human needs.

Fire

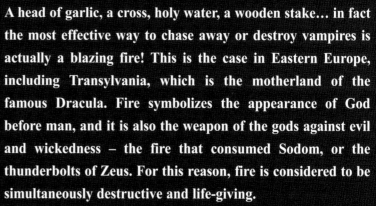

A head of garlic, a cross, holy water, a wooden stake... in fact the most effective way to chase away or destroy vampires is actually a blazing fire! This is the case in Eastern Europe, including Transylvania, which is the motherland of the famous Dracula. Fire symbolizes the appearance of God before man, and it is also the weapon of the gods against evil and wickedness – the fire that consumed Sodom, or the thunderbolts of Zeus. For this reason, fire is considered to be simultaneously destructive and life-giving.

In Eastern Europe, it was the custom to burn people suspected of being vampires (in a similar way to that in which people were burned as witches by the Catholic Inquisition). When they wanted to expel the vampire from a particular region, they would surround the region with blazing bonfires. Sometimes, the bonfires formed a cross. According to an ancient tale from Russia, a vampire was tempted to approach the blacksmith's furnace by means of a plateful of blood, and when he bent over the plate, he was pushed into the fiery furnace. This motif of destroying vampires by fire appears in many books whose heroes are vampires (or the vampire-slayer).

The Vampyre

From the drear mansions of the tomb,

From the low regions of the dead,

The ghost of Sigismund doth roam,

And dreadful haunts me in my bed!

There vested in infernal guise,

By means to me not understood,

Close to my side the goblin lies,

And drinks away my vital blood!

John Stagg (1810)

Baital-Pachisi

Everyone in the West is familiar with the name of Dracula, and everyone associates it with vampires. But who knows the name of Baital? And how is he connected to vampires?

Baital is the name of the most famous vampire in the East, especially in India. He is a large and threatening vampire, an evil spirit that reveals itself in dead bodies. This Baital is the hero of many Hindu legends that were written in Sanskrit and are reminiscent of the stories of the One Thousand and One Nights.

The stories of the Baital reached the West when the renowned Captain Sir Richard Burton translated the book, Baital-Pachisi, into English in 1870 and called it *King Vikram and the Vampire*. Vikram was a warrior king who was given a mission: to bring the vampire from the city to the wizard (Jogi). The accomplishment of this mission entailed adventures, magic, and a romantic atmosphere, which combine to form an enchanting adventure story, during the course of which the vampire appears over and over again. These vampire stories – the most widespread stories in the East – won the hearts of Western readers as soon as they were translated into English.

On this page we can see the illustrations of Ernest Griset and Albert Letchford, which appeared in the edition of the book that was published in 1893.

Vampires

I will destroy the gates of hell,
confusion will reign among the beings of the
depths and those of the surface
The dead turn up, they are fed like the living.
The legions of the dead will be more numerous
than those of the living.

The Epic of Gilgamesh

Vampires in China

When scholars from the West began to study Chinese folklore, they came across the legend of the *kiang-shi*, the Chinese vampire. His existence derived from the Chinese belief in the existence of two souls. This belief stated that every person has a superior soul, which is rational, and an inferior soul, which is not rational. The superior soul assumes the shape of the body, and during the time of separation between body and soul – the moment of death – this soul appears in another form, generally that of an animal. After death, it has the ability to leave the body and wander around, and then take control of another body and speak through it. If it has accidents, these are liable to have negative effects on the body.

The inferior soul, which is called *p'ai* or *p'o*, is the soul that resides in the fetus during pregnancy. In general, this soul also remains in the dead body and accompanies it during the transition to supernatural existence. At the moment of death, when the soul leaves, the body disintegrates entirely. If the p'o is strong enough, it can remain in the dead body for a long period of time and use it until it has completely disintegrated. Such a body becomes the kiang-shi or the vampire. In certain cases, it appears as a shining green light, and in others, it receives the ghastly appearance of a creature with long teeth and nails. The kiang-shi is identified with violent death, and occurs as a result of suicide, hanging or drowning. Furthermore, it can occur in a person who died suddenly or was buried incorrectly. If the burial is delayed for too long, the deceased can become angry and restless, and then turn into a kiang-shi. Animals, especially cats, are kept far away from the body so that they do not jump on it and become vampires as well. The existence of kiang-shi begins as an unburied corpse, but after a certain period, the kiang-shi gains strength and becomes mobile. They get out of the coffin, learn how to fly and become covered with white hair. In certain cases, they are liable to turn into wolves.

The kiang-shi vampires are strong and cruel. The texts say that they would attack living people and tear their heads and limbs off while they were still alive. Since they do not have the seductive powers of the Western vampire, the only thing they can do is surprise their victims, in this way gaining an advantage over them. Their highly developed sexual drive causes them to attack and rape women. Just like in the West, protection against them takes the form of garlic and salt, which cause the kiang-shi to keep their distance. They shy away from loud noises, and thunder can even kill them with its intensity. A broom is an effective weapon for anyone who is brave enough to confront the kiang-shi. It is customary to sprinkle rice and red lentils around the coffin of the deceased in order to keep the kiang-shi away. If the kiang-shi has already turned into a hairy flying creature, only thunder or a bullet can bring him down. The ultimate solution for getting rid of the kiang-shi is fire. Only fire has purifying powers, and only by burning the kiang-shi completely can its possible return to life be avoided.

After World War II, the Chinese vampire got a new lease on life with the development of the movie industry in Hong Kong and Taiwan. During the 1950s and 1960s, two vampire movies were produced in Malaysia, one of them *Vampire Woman* (*Xi Xuefu*) in 1962, which tells the story of a woman who was accused of being a vampire and executed by burning after drinking the blood of her baby. The tragedy depicted in this movie was that after her death, it was discovered that the baby had been poisoned and she was actually try to save its life by trying to suck out the poisoned blood. Another movie with a vampire theme, *Vampire Kung-fu*, came out in 1972, and a year later, the great horror movie, *The Legend of the Seven Golden Vampires*, reached the screen. In addition, there was a movie called *The Seven Brothers Meet Dracula*, which transferred the Dracula story to China. It featured seven vampires that protect themselves by means of their expertise in the martial arts.

Vampires in ancient Rome and in Italy

nlike Greece, ancient Rome did not contribute a single entity of its own to the well-known vampire myth. The ones that existed in ancient Rome were mainly live witches rather than creatures that returned from the dead. As we have already mentioned, the notion of a vampiric entity came from ancient Greece in the form of the lamiai, and it was used as a response to the question of the unexplained death of many infants.

The Romans had the *strix*, a nocturnal creature that attacked infants and sucked their blood. It was identified with the screech owl, and was called *striges* in Greece, *strigoi* in Romania, and subsequently *strega* throughout Italy. Generally, this was a woman who was believed to turn into a bird at night. It was also believed that her breath was poisonous, and that she had the power to suck the blood of innocent human beings. The strega continued to be a part of the popular Roman culture and reached every corner of the ancient Roman Empire. At the end of the ninth century, Charlemagne – who created the Holy Roman Empire – declared that anyone who accused anyone else of being a strega would be punished. For 600 years, many people were careful of the strega. At the end of the 15th century, thanks to the Inquisition, witches had been demonized, and the struggle with the devil was carried out through them. Anyone who was accused of being a strega was arrested, tortured, and put to death in Italy during the period of the infamous witch-hunts. During the interrogation of women suspected of being witches, the inquisitors forced them to confess to strega practices, which included, among other things, turning infants into vampires, and they were sentenced to death by burning.

Between the years 1460 and 1525, ten books about witchcraft were published. One of the volumes relates to the strega and the strix, and it contains texts on witchcraft that was practiced in Brecia in 1518 and in Sondrio in 1523. The picture described by the writer, Mirandola, was more complete than the records of the trials of the women who were accused of acts of demonic sorcery. Mirandola's beliefs persisted throughout the Renaissance and were even predominant among the religious and intellectual leaders in subsequent centuries.

When the vampire plague struck Serbia and the other Eastern European countries in the 17th century, the phenomenon reached the modern world, that is, Italy. The Franciscan from Pavia, Ludovico Maria Sinistrari, decided to include the vampire phenomenon in a study of satanic phenomena, and even proposed a theological interpretation that was very different than the rational explanations that would emerge in Europe just a short time later. Sinistrari thought that the vampires were creatures that did not evolve from the first man, that is, they were not human at all, while their soul was rational, like that of human beings. This fact caused them to resemble humans more than differ from them.

Thanks to the more modern interpretation of J. H. Zedler in 1745, it was possible to discard Sinistrari's somewhat sinister opinions. Zedler claimed that the belief in vampires was nothing but a superstition and a man-made attempt to explain the outbreaks of plague in Europe. Two years previously, in 1743, Cardinal Giuseppe Davanzati had already claimed that the belief in vampires only existed in the isolated regions of Europe, and that vampires were none other than the fruit of the peasants' imagination. He maintained that the fact that the belief in vampires did not exist in the large and enlightened cities of Eastern Europe reinforced his claim.

Pope Benedict XIV was pleased with Davanzati's opinion, as

was Prospero Lambertini, who wrote the text that later served as the basic Roman Catholic source regarding miracles and the supernatural for many years. Like the pope, Lambertini also threatened to take punitive measures against the Polish bishops who were overly forthcoming about their belief in vampires, as he claimed.

In the mid-18th century, there were numerous reports of the existence of vampires in Central and Eastern Europe. In

1749, the French Benedictine scholar, Dom Augustin Calmet, wrote a report that became the source of inspiration for vampire novels in the following centuries. In 1755, Gerhard van Swieten wrote a treatise according to which vampirism was simply a superstition that was based on ignorance. This marked the victory of scientific rationalism, which later dominated the culture of the late 18th century.

At the beginning of the 19th century, the first literary works about vampires began to appear, mainly in Northern Europe. Traditional vampire literature began in Italy with De Gasperini's opera, *Il Vampiro*, which was first staged in Turin in 1801. The Romantic movement itself, which had numerous supporters and described the inner human experience in detail, advocated a mythical figure of a vampire by highlighting the symbols "blood", "night" and "melancholy", as well as a "delicate and erotic approach to corpses". In this way, the inhabitants of the big cities were introduced to vampires mainly through the works of Novalis, Goethe and Keats. John Polidori's book about the famous vampire, Lord Ruthven, was written in 1819, but it was not translated into Italian prior to the 20th century. Vampires began to appear mainly in French and Russian literature, in the works of Baudelaire, Dumas, Tolstoy and Gogol.

The first Romantic novel to be published in Italy, *Il Vampiro*, was written by Franco Mistrali, and appeared in 1869. The plot unfolded in Monaco in 1862 and focused on blood and incest. It presents the vampire as a decadent literary figure with aristocratic mores that was almost certainly influenced by the European literature of the period, including the works of

Keats, Goethe, Polidori and Byron. The historical and folkloristic connotations of the vampire, as they were documented during the plague of vampires, became the central topic of the novel *Vampiro* that was written by Enrico Boni in 1908. This was possibly the only work that presented the world of superstition and fear that existed in the rural culture.

At the end of the 19th century and the beginning of the 20th century, with the development of modern Italian poetry, vampires found their place in two avant-garde art movements: the Scapigliatura and Futurism. The central theme was the vamp, the seductive female vampire, when she appears in her most erotic and aggressive dimension and is described in images that were taken mainly from the late Romantic period and from French poetry (especially that of Baudelaire).

After the decline of those movements, 20th-century Italian poetry and literature hardly drew on the vampire myth. Halfway through the century, vampires barely featured in the works of Italy's leading authors, such as Aldo Palazzeschi and Dino Campana. However, in the 1970s, the lamiai – the ancient Greek vampire – featured in Giovanni Fontana's book, and this helped to develop the metaphoric, artistic and poetic role of the vampire.

Many Italians were exposed to vampires through the comics that began to appear in the 1960s, some of them translated from English, but most of them were original and presented new characters with their own plots. Among them is Jacula, the comic female vampire, who managed to survive 327 issues over a period of 14 years – from 1969 to 1982. Her success engendered many attempts at imitation, but only *Zora* enjoyed a comparable success, with 235 issues over a period of 12 years – from 1973 to 1985. While the Italian comic books related mainly to Dracula, they also related to other aristocratic Eastern European vampires, such as Zagor, who was produced in the 1970s. At the end of the 1990s, the Italian vampire comic books were more popular than ever.

In 1982, Furio Jesi published short stories for children featuring a playful vampire. His main contribution, however, lies in his book, *The Last Night*, where he described vampires as mythical archetypes that symbolize life, and whose mission is to reconquer the earth and the human race, which is well on the way to ecological destruction.

In 1984, Alberto Abruzzese created an interesting symbolic interpretation of the figure of the vampire and completely broke with tradition. This time, the story was about a high official in the communist party who discovered that his true identity was that of a vampire. This revelation came about as a result of the psychological changes he was undergoing because of various fears. The protagonist finally accepts the change and regains balance in his life. In this case, the vampire myth served as an allegory about the difficulties experienced by the old Italian party when it came to adapting itself to the new post-communist Democratic Party.

The vampires regained their old identity in 1987 in Gianfranco Manfredi's series of novels, in which the last surviving vampires describe their centuries-long historical attempt to live alongside human beings and imitate their behavior, but are ultimately defeated by them. In this way, Manfredi succeeded in describing several historical events – among them the Lutheran Reformation and the Spanish Inquisition – in an interesting manner and from the vampires' point of view.

In the literature of the 1980s, the vampire was endowed with a Western European and North American style rather than an Italian style. Many of the novels that had been written in English were now translated into Italian. Despite this, the Italians did not stop writing about vampires in their own popular works as well as in more serious novels. Among the more promising Italian writers who contributed to this tradition, we can find Patrizia Valduga, who wrote the novel *Donna di Dolori* (*Woman of Pain*) in 1991. The book features vampires in order to remind the reader of all the atrocities that were perpetrated during the 20th century.

In the 1990s, important studies about the vampire phenomenon were conducted in Italy. In 1995, Massimo Introvigne, a scholar of religious studies and Dracula researcher, founded the Italian branch of the Transylvanian Society of Dracula.

In the movie industry, successful vampire movies began to be produced in 1957 with Riccardo Freda's movie, followed by Stefano Steno's movie two years later. In the 1960s, Mario Bava conquered the big screen with his horror movies, and as a result, a new wave of vampire horror movies began, inspired, among other things, by vampire books that became successful series. This is how the sophisticated vampire emerged in novels such as those of Luigi Pellizzetti and Italo Calvino. The traditional stereotype of the vampire was exchanged for a more metaphorical and complex figure.

About Transylvania

*T*ransylvania was the region that was most closely identified with the existence of vampires. The literal translation of the name is "the land beyond the forest", and it is situated in the central and northern part of Romania. According to Bram Stoker, who described the country as beautiful, wild and unknown, Castle Dracula is located there. Although the location of the castle – according to the novel – does not appear on any map, and although it seems like an imaginary place, Transylvania is completely real.

In the first century AD, Transylvania was an attractive region that had been partially conquered by Trajan in 106. During the following several centuries, the Romanian people began to emerge there. They aligned themselves with the Eastern Orthodox church whose center was in Constantinople, even though the first Christian missionaries had already arrived there. Over the centuries, there were attempts by various peoples to invade and conquer Transylvania. The most important of these were the Hungarians, who occupied the region in the 10th century. Three hundred years later, Hungary claimed control over Transylvania, even though various divisions were ruled by local territorial lords. The Hungarians effected some social changes, such as convincing the Szekely people, who turned out to be great warriors and lived in the west of Transylvania, to migrate to the mountainous region in the east in order to protect the border there. In order to improve the economic situation in the region, the Hungarians invited Germans to settle in the south of Transylvania in exchange for generous tax benefits. These people constituted the beginning of the Saxon people, and they controlled the mountain passes linking Transylvania and Wallachia.

In the 14th century, there were four principal peoples living in Transylvania: the Hungarians, the Hungarian-speaking Szekelys, the Saxons and the Romanians. When the Hungarians tried to impose Roman Catholicism on all the other peoples, many Romanians, who had constituted the majority in the region until then and were not particularly loyal to the Hungarian crown, preferred to cross the mountains into Moldavia and Wallachia. In the 15th century, an ongoing battle was waged on two fronts – against the Hungarians from the north and the Turks from the south, both of whom wanted to seize control of the region.

In 1436, Vlad Dracul ascended to the throne of Wallachia, where he brought a great deal of pride to his people. In 1447, he decided to confront John Hunyadi, governor of Transylvania and his arch-rival, and was killed. Hunyadi remained in power until his death in 1456, when Dracul's son, known as Vlad the Impaler, succeeded to the throne. As the ruler of Wallachia, Vlad the Impaler conquered additional territories. Before Hunyadi died, however, he championed the cause of his own son, who became the king of Hungary in 1458.

Vlad the Impaler was in fact the historic Dracula. Writer Bram Stoker derived his inspiration from him and decided to place him in North-East Transylvania, perhaps because in spite of his being the ruler of Wallachia, Vlad's country of origin was none other than Transylvania.

Today, Transylvania serves as a major tourist attraction, and boasts ski resorts and wine. Numerous hotels in the region have adopted names and concepts from the successful novel, *Dracula*, and this seems to enhance their success with tourists.

The hyena male after seven years becomes a bat, the bat after seven years becomes a Vampire, the Vampire after seven years becomes a nettle, the nettle after seven years becomes a sloe, the sloe after seven years transforms into a demon.

Talmud.

Witchcraft and Vampirism.

"Oh, friend and partner of the night, who becomes enraptured with dogs howling to intimidate their prey, who worships the running blood, you wander among the shadows between the tombstones and make mortals tremble! Gorgo, Mormo, the thousand faces of the Moon, value our sacrifices.

H. P Lovecraft

Acting within this book is a "subterranean" being, of those who go deeper, who corrupt, who undermine. If we have eyes capable of reaching such depth, we see him progressing slowly, prudently, with inflexible softness, without denouncing too much the anguish that follows light and air privation. We can say that we are satisfied in accomplishing this somber work. Does it not seem guided by some sort of faith and compensated for any consolation? He wishes perhaps to know deep darkness, his incomprehensible secret, enigmatic element, for he knows very well what he will receive in return: his redemption, his aurora. No doubt he will come back to the surface: do not ask him what you search for down there, he will tell you himself – a subterranean animal of Trophonius appearance, once again "he becomes man". We completely forget the silence when, like him, we were buried for so long and isolated.

I will tell you, patient friends, what I searched for down there. I will tell you that it could have been a last goodbye, a funeral prayer, for I came back and I am here. Do not even think for a moment that I intend to suggest you do the same! Nor that you experience the same loneliness! For the one who goes his own way does not meet anybody: this is essential to the nature of "his own way". No one comes to help him in his undertaking - he must overcome danger, threat, wickedness and storms - everything that assails him must be faced alone. It is because his way lies in himself, naturally.

Nietzsche

Werewolves

The werewolf is another of the monsters devised by the human brain, and is associated with the vampire. The link between werewolves and vampires was created in the 1930s, when two movies about werewolves were screened. In these movies, the werewolf was portrayed as a person who, at certain times – particularly on nights with a full moon – would change into a wolf or into something wolf-like either voluntarily or against his will. He would assume characteristics of the wolf – especially its evil and cruel nature. In the myths of many different cultures, it has been found that werewolves and vampires generally existed side by side. In the southern Balkan region, especially in Greece, the *vrykolakas* appeared. At the beginning of the 20th century, they were actually identified as a type of werewolf.

Since the vampire itself is a nocturnal creature, it can be supposed that it has a special affinity for the moon, as described in John Polidori's book, *The Vampire* (1819), when the moon rose and shone in the heavens after the death of the vampire, Lord Ruthven. This notion prevailed in the vampire stories that were written in the first half of the 19th century. However, Bram Stoker used the moon for the sole purpose of creating an atmosphere, without any supernatural qualities that affect vampires. In contrast, the werewolf, as we have mentioned, is directly affected by the moon and its movements.

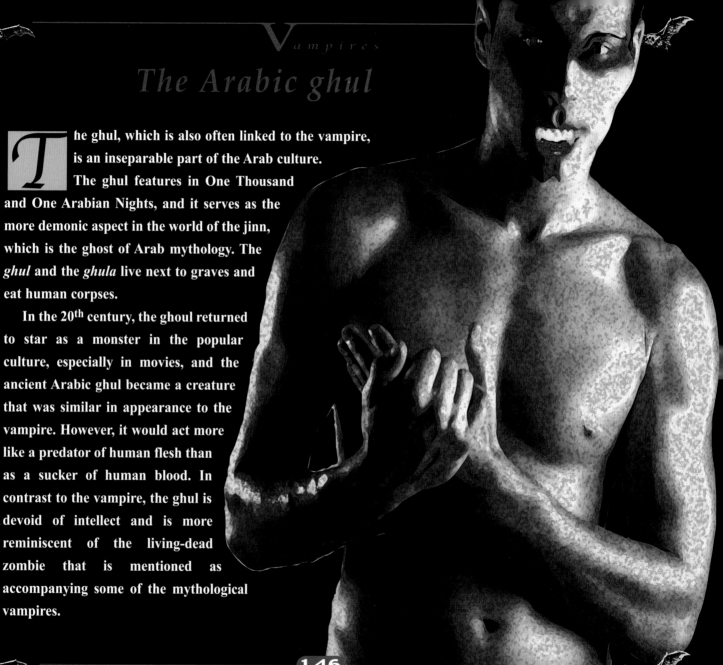

The Arabic ghul

The ghul, which is also often linked to the vampire, is an inseparable part of the Arab culture. The ghul features in One Thousand and One Arabian Nights, and it serves as the more demonic aspect in the world of the jinn, which is the ghost of Arab mythology. The *ghul* and the *ghula* live next to graves and eat human corpses.

In the 20th century, the ghoul returned to star as a monster in the popular culture, especially in movies, and the ancient Arabic ghul became a creature that was similar in appearance to the vampire. However, it would act more like a predator of human flesh than as a sucker of human blood. In contrast to the vampire, the ghul is devoid of intellect and is more reminiscent of the living-dead zombie that is mentioned as accompanying some of the mythological vampires.

The victims of the vampires

According to the experience and opinion of the vampire hunter, Dr. Abraham Van Helsinger, who features in Bram Stoker's novel, Dracula, vampires have no conscience. The vampire swoops down on the bodies and souls of those we love most. However, according to folkloristic and cultural history, it turns out that the vampire also swoops down on the ones he loves most. According to the testimonies, the vampires generally came back in order to kill the ones among whom they had lived, including all those people they had loved when they were alive. This fact constitutes the main difference between the traditional vampire and the literary vampire that emerged in the 19th century. The traditional vampire was an inseparable part of rural culture and limited himself to the cemetery area or the village houses where his victims, the villagers, lived. In contrast, the literary protagonists were citizens of the big wide world. Another difference lies in the belief of the victim. The folkloristic vampire sometimes attacked randomly and would turn his victims into vampires themselves. The literary vampire of the 19th century usually attacked his victims, sucked their blood, sapped their energy, but did not kill them outright. When the victim himself became a vampire, the vampire and his victim shared each other's blood, and this is how the transformation took place.

During the last generation, a new vampire was born: the good vampire, which refrains from killing people. These are vampires that seek blood in the blood bank or prefer to make do with the blood of animals. If they have no choice but to attack human beings, they opt for bad and corrupt ones rather than innocent and kindhearted ones. St. Germain, Chelsea Quinn Yarbro's vampire protagonist, was like that. He would even pleasure his victim sexually, and if he could prevent his victim from becoming a vampire, he would do so happily.

Pages from Dracula by Bram Stoker

... 24 June, before morning. – Last night the Count left me early, and locked himself into his own room. As soon as I dared, I ran up the winding staiyttr, and looked out of the window which opened south. I thought I would watch for the Count, for there is something going on. The Szgany are quartered somewhere in the castle, and are doing work of some kind. I know it, for now and then I hear a far-away, muffled sound as of mattock and spade, and, whatever it is, it must be to the end of some ruthless villainy.

I had been at the window somewhat less than half an hour, when I saw something coming out of the Count's window. I drew back and watched carefully, and saw the whole man emerge. It was a new chock to me to find that he had on the suit of clothes which I had worn whilst traveling here, and slung over his shoulder the terrible bag which I had seen the women take away. There could be no doubt as to his quest, and in my garb, too! This, then is his new scheme of evil: that he will allow others to see me, as they think, so that he may both leave evidence that I have been seen in the towns or villages posting my own letters, and that any wickedness which he may do shall by the local people be attributed to me.

It makes me rage to think that this can go on, and whilst I am shut up here, a veritable prisoner, but without that protection of the law which is even a criminal's right and consolation.

I thought I would watch for the count's return, and for a long time sat doggedly at the window. Then I began to notice that there were some quaint little specks floating in the rays of the moonlight. They were like the tiniest grains of dust, and they whirled round and gathered in clusters in a nebulous sort of way. I watched them with a sense of soothing, and a sort of calm stole over me. I leaned back in the embrasure in a more comfortable position, so that I could enjoy more fully the aerial gamboling.

Something made me start up, a low piteous howling of dogs somewhere far below in the valley, which was hidden from my sight. Louder it seemed to ring in my ears, and the floating motes of dust to take new shapes to the sound as they danced in the moonlight. I felt myself struggling to awake to some call of my instincts; nay, my very soul was struggling, and my half-remembered sensibilities were striving to answer the call. I was becoming hypnotized! Quicker and quicker danced the dust, and the moonbeams seemed to quiver as they went by me into the mass of gloom beyond. More and more they gathered till they seemed to take dim phantom shapes. And then I started, broad awake and in full possession of my senses, and ran screaming from the place. The phantom shapes, which were becoming gradually materialized from the moonbeams, were those of the three ghostly women to whom I was doomed. I fled, and felt somewhat safer in my own room, where there was no moonlight and where the lamp was burning brightly.

When a couple of hours had passed I heard something stirring in the Count's room, something like a sharp wail quickly suppressed; and then there was a silence, deep, awful silence, which chilled me. With a beating heart, I tried the door; but I was locked in my prison, and could do nothing. I sat down and simply cried.

As I sat I heard a sound in the courtyard without – the agonized cry of a woman. I rushed to the window, and throwing it up, peered out between the bars. There, indeed, was a woman with disheveled hair, holding her hands over her heart as one distressed with running. She was leaning against a corner of the gateway. When she saw my face at the window she threw herself forward, and shouted in a voice laden with menace: —

"Monster, give me my child!"

She threw herself on her knees, and raising up her hands, cried the same words in tones which wrung my heart. Then she tore her hair and beat her breast, and abandoned herself to all the violences of extravagant emotion. Finally, she threw herself forward, and, though I could not see her, I could hear the beating of her naked hands against the door.

Somewhere high overhead, probably on the tower, I heard the voice of the Count calling in his harsh, metallic whisper. His call seemed to be answered from far and wide by the howling of wolves. Before many minutes had passed a pack of them poured, like a pent-up dam when liberated, through the wide entrance into the courtyard.

There was no cry from the woman, and the howling of the wolves was but short. Before long they streamed away singly, licking their lips.

I could not pity her, for I knew now what had become of her child, and she was better dead.

What shall I do? What can I do? How can I escape from this dreadful thrall of night and gloom and fear?

25 June, morning – No man knows till he has suffered from the night how sweet and how dear to his heart and eye the morning can be. When the sun grew so high this morning that it struck the top of the great gateway opposite my window, the high spot which it touched seemed to me as if the dove from the ark had lighted there. My fear fell from me as if it had been a vaporous garment which dissolved in the warmth. I must take action of some sort while the courage of the day is upon me. Last night one of my post-dated letters went to post, the first of that fatal series which is to blot out the very traces of my existence from the earth.

Let me not think of it. Action!

It has always been at night-time that I have been molested or threatened, or in some way in danger or in fear. I have not yet seen the Count in the daylight. Can it be that he sleeps when others wake, that he may be awake whilst they sleep! If I could only get into his room! But there is no possible way. The door is always locked, no way for me.

Yes, there is a way, if one dares to take it. When his body has gone why may not another body go? I have seen him myself crawl from his window; why should not I imitate him, and go in by his window? The chances are desperate, but my need is more desperate still. I shall risk it. At the worst it can only be death. And a man's death is not a calf's, and the dread Hereafter may still be open to me. God help me in my task! Good-by, Mina, if I fail: good-by, my faithful friend and second father; good-bye, all, and last of all Mina!

Same day, later. – I have made the effort, and, God helping me, have come safely back to this room. I must put down every detail in order. I went whilst my courage was fresh straight to the window on the south side, and at once got outside on the narrow ledge of stone which runs round the building on this side. The stones were big and roughly cut, and the mortar had by process of time been washed away between them. I took off my boots, and ventured out on the desperate way. I looked down once, so as to make sure that sudden glimpse of the awful depth would not overcome me, but after that kept my eyes away from it. I knew pretty well the directions and distance of the Count's window, and made for it as well as I could, having regard to the opportunities available. I did not feel dizzy – I suppose I was too excited – and the time seemed ridiculously short till I found myself standing on the window-sill and trying to raise up the sash. I was filled with agitation, however, when I bent down and slid feet foremost in through the window. Then I looked around for the Count but, with surprise and gladness, made a discovery. The room was empty! It was barely furnished with odd things, which seemed to have never been used; the furniture was something the same style as that in the south rooms, and was covered with dust. I looked for the key, but it was not in the lock, and I could not find it anywhere. The only thing I found was a great heap of gold in one corner – gold of all kinds, Roman, and British, and Austrian, and Hungarian, and Greek and Turkish money, covered with a film of dust, as though it had lain long in the ground. None of it that I noticed was less than three hundred years old. There were also chains and ornaments, some jeweled, but all of them old and stained.

At one corner of the room was a heavy door. I tried it, for since I could not find the key of the room or the key of the outer door, which was the main object of my search, I must make further examination, or all my efforts would be in vain. It was open, and led through a stone passage to a circular stairway, which went steely down. I descended, minding carefully where I went, for the stairs were dark, being only lit by loopholes in the heavy masonry. At the bottom there was a dark, tunnel-like passage, through which came a deathly, sickly odor, the odor of old earth newly turned. As I went through the passage the smell grew closer and heavier. At last I pulled open a heavy door which stood ajar, and found myself in an old, ruined chapel, which had evidently been used as a graveyard, The roof was broken, and in two places were steps leading to vaults, but the ground had recently been dug over, and the earth placed in great wooden boxes, manifestly those which had been brought by the Slovaks. There was nobody about, and I made search for any further outlet, but there was none. Then I went over every inch of the ground, so as not to lose a chance. I went down even into the vaults, where the dim light struggled, although to do so was a dread to my very soul. Into two of these I went, but saw nothing except fragments of old coffins and piles of dust; in the third, however, I made a discovery.

There, in one of the great boxes, of which there were fifty in all, on a pile of newly dug earth, lay the Count! He was either dead of asleep, I could not say which – for the eyes were open and stony, but without the glassiness of death – and the cheeks had the warmth of life through all their pallor, and the lips were as red as ever. But there was no sign of movement, no pulse, no breath, no beating of the heart. I bent over him, and tried to find any sign of life, but in vain. He could not have lain there long, for the earthy smell would have passed away in a few hours. By the side of the box was its cover, pierced with holes here and there. I thought he might have the keys on him, but when I went to search I saw the dead eyes, and in them, dead though they were, such a look of hate, though unconscious of me or my presence, that I fled from the place, and leaving the Count's room by the window, crawled again up the castle wall. Regaining my own chamber, I threw myself panting upon the bed and tried to think….

30 September. – When we met in Dr. Seward's study two hours after dinner, which had been at six o'clock, we unconsciously formed a sort of board or committee. Professor Van Helsing took the head of the table, to which Dr. Seward motioned him as he came into the room. He made me sit next to him on his right, and asked me to act as secretary Jonathan sat next to me. Opposite us were Lord Godalming, Dr. Seward and Mr. Morris – Lord Godalming being next the Professor and Dr. Seward in the centre. The Professor said: –

"I may, I suppose, take it that we are all acquainted with the facts that are in these papers." We all expressed assent, and he went on: –

"Then it were, I think, good that I tell you something of the kind of enemy with which we have to deal. I shall then make known to you something of the history of this man, which has been ascertained for me. So we then can discuss how we shall act, and can take our measure according.

"There are such beings as vampires; some of us have evidence that they exist. Even had we not the proof of our own unhappy experience, the teaching and the records o the past give proof enough for sane peoples. I admit that at the first I was sceptic. Were it not that through long years I have trained myself to keep an open mind, I could not have believed until such time as that fact thunder on my ear: 'See! See! I prove; I prove.' Alas! Had I known at the first what now I know – nay, had I even guess at him – one so precious life had been spared to many of us who did love her. But that is gone; and we must so work that other poor souls perish not, whilst we can save. The nosferatu do not die like the bee when he sting once. He is only stronger; and being stronger, have yet more power to work evil. This vampire which is amongst us is of himself so strong in person as twenty me; he is of cunning more than mortal, for his cunning be the growth of ages; he have still the aids of necromancy, which is, as his etymology imply, the divination by the dead, and all the dead that he can come nigh to are for him at command; he is brute, and more than brute; he is devil in callous, and the heart of him is not; he can, within his range, direct the elements: the storm, the fog, the thunder: he can command all the meaner thing: the rat, and the owl, and the bat – the moth, and the fox, and the wolf; he can grow and become small; and he can at times vanish and come unknown. How then are we to begin our strife to destroy him? How shall we find his where; and having found it, how can we destroy? My friends, this is much; it is a terrible task that we undertake, and there may be consequence to make the brave shudder. For if we fail in this our fight we must surely win: and then where end we? Life is nothing! I heed him not. But to fail here is not mere life of death. It is that we come as him; that we henceforward become foul things of the night like him – without heart or conscience, preying on the bodies and the souls of those we love best. To us for ever are the gates of heaven shut; for who shall open them to us again? We go on for all time abhorred by all; a blot on the face of God's sunshine; an arrow in the side of Him who died for man. But we are face to face with duty; and in such case must we shrink? For me, I say, no; but then I am old, and life, with his sunshine, his fair places, his song of birds, his music, and his love, life far behind. You others are young. Some have seen sorrow; but there are fair days yet in store. What say you?

Whilst he was speaking Jonathan had taken my hand. I feared, oh so much, that the appalling nature of our danger was overcoming him when I saw his hand stretch out; but it was life to me to feel its touch – so strong, so self-reliant, so resolute. A brave man's hand can speak for itself; it does not even need a woman's love to hear its music.

When the Professor had done speaking my husband looked in my eyes, and I in his; there was no need for speaking between us.

"I answer for Mina and myself," he said.

"Count me in, Professor," said Mr Quincey Morris, laconically as usual.

"I am with you," said Lord Godalming, "For Lucy's sake, if for no other reason."

Dr. Seward simply nodded. The Professor stood up, and, after laying his golden crucifix on the table, held out his hand on either side. I took his right hand, and Lord Godalming his left; Jonathan held my right with his left and stretched across to Mr. Morris. So as we all took hands our solemn compact was made. I felt my heart icy cold, but it did not even occur to me to draw back. We resumed our places, and Dr. Van Helsing went on with a sort of cheerfulness which showed that the serious work had begun. It was to be taken as gravely, and in as businesslike a way, as any other transaction of life: –

"Well, you know what we have to contend against; but we, too, are not without strength. We have on our side power of combination – a power denied to the vampire kind; we have resources of science; we are free to act and think; and the hours of the day and the night are ours equally. In fact, so far as our powers extend, they are unfettered, and we are free to use them. We have self-devotion in a cause, and an end to achieve which is not a selfish one. These things are much.

"Now let us see how far the general powers arrayed against us are restrict, and how the individual cannot. In fine, let us consider the limitations of the vampire in general, and of this one in particular.

"All we have to go upon are traditions and superstitions. These do not at the first appear much, when the matter is one of life and earth – nay, of more than either life or death. Yet must we be satisfied; in the first place because we have to be – no other means is at our control – and secondly, because, after all, these things – tradition and superstition – are everything. Does not the belief in vampires rest for others – though no, alas! For us – on them? A year ago which of us would have received such a possibility, in the midst of our scientific skeptical, matter of fact nineteenth century? We even scouted a belief that we saw justified under of very eyes. Take it, then, that the vampire, and the belief in his limitations and his cure, rest for the moment on the same base. For, let me tell you, he is known everywhere that men have been. In old Greece, in old Rome; he flourish in Germany all over, in France, in India, even in the Chersonese; and in China, so far from us in all ways, there even is he, and the peoples fear him at this day. He have followed the wake of the berserker Icelander, the devil-begotten Hun, the Slav, the Saxon, the Magyar. So far, then we have all we may act upon; and let me tell you that very much of the beliefs are justified by what we have seen in our own so unhappy experience. The vampire lives on, and cannot die by mere passing of the time; he can flourish when that he can fatten on the blood of the living. Even more, we have seen amongst us that he can even grow younger; that his vital faculties grow strenuous, and seem as though they refresh themselves when his special pabulum is plenty. But he cannot flourish without this diet; he eat not as others. Even friend Jonathan, who lived with him for weeks, did never see him to eat, never! He throws no shadow; he make in the mirror no reflect, as again Jonathan observe. He has the strength of many in his hand – witness again Jonathan when he shut the door against the wolves, and when he help him from the diligence too. He can transform himself to wolf, as we gather from the ship arrival in Whitby, when he tear open the dog; he can be as bat, as Madam Mina saw him on the window at Whitby, and as friend John saw him fly from this so near house, and as my friend Quincey saw him at the window of Miss Lucy. He can come in mist which he create – that noble ship's captain proved him of this; but, from what we know, the distance he can make this mist is limited, and it can only be round himself. He come on moonlight rays as elemental dust – as again Jonathan saw those sister in the castle of Dracula. He become so small – we ourselves saw Miss Lucy, ere she was at peace, slip through a hair-breadth space at the tomb door. He can, when once he find his way, come out from anything or into anything, no matter how close it be bound or even fused up with fire – solder you call it. He can see in the dark – no small power this, in a world which is one half shut from the light. Ah, but hear me through. He can do all these things, yet he is not free. Nay, he is even more prisoner than the slave of the galley, than the madman in his cell. He cannot go where he lists; he who is not of nature has yet to obey some of nature's laws – why we know not. He may not enter anywhere at the first, unless there be someone of the household who bid him to come; though afterwards he can come as he please. His power ceases, as does that of all evil things, at the coming of the day. Only at certain times can he have limited freedom. If he be not at the place whither he is bound, he can only change himself at noon or at exact sunrise or sunset. These things are we told, and in this record of ours we have proof by inference. Thus, whereas he can do as he will within his limit, when he have his earth-home, his coffin-home, his hell-home, the place unhallowed, as we saw when he went to the grave of the suicide at Whitby; still at other time he can only change when the time come. It is said, too, that he can only pass running water at the slack or the flood of the tide. Then there are things which so afflict him that he has no power, as the garlic that we know of, and as for things sacred, as this symbol, my crucifix, that was amongst us even now when we resolve, to them he is nothing, but in their presence he take his place far off and silent with respect. There are others, too which I shall tell you of, lest in our seeking we may need them. The branch of wild rose on his coffin keep him that he move not from it; a sacred bullet fired into the coffin kill him so that he be true dead; and as for the stake through him, we know already of its peace; or the cut-off head that giveth rest. We have seen it with our eyes.

"Thus when we find the habitation of this man-that-was, we can confine him to his coffin and destroy him, if we obey what we know. But he is clever. I have asked my friend Arminius, of Buda-Pesth University, to make his record; and, from all the means that are, he tell me of what he has been. He must, indeed, have been that Voivode Dracula who won his name against the Turk, over the great river on the very frontier of Turkey-land. If it be so, then was he no common man; for in that time, and for centuries after, he was spoken of as the cleverest and the most cunning, as well as the bravest of the sons of the "land beyond the forest." That mighty brain and that iron resolution went with him to his grave, and are even now arrayed against us. The Draculas were, says Arminius, a great and noble race, though now and again were scions who were held by their coevals to have had dealings with the Evil One. They learned his secrets in the Scholomance, amongst the mountains over Lake Hermanstadt, where the devil claims the tenth scholar as his due. In the records are such words as "stregoica" – which; "ordog" and "pokol" – Satan and hell; and in one manuscript this very Dracula is spoken of as "wamyr," which we all understand too well. There have been from the loins of this very one great men and good women,

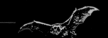

and their graves make sacred the earth where alone this foulness can dwell. For it is not the least of its terrors that this evil thing is rooted deep in all good; in soil barren holy memories it cannot rest."

Whilst they were talking Mr. Morris was looking steadily at the window, and he now got up quietly, and went out of the room. There was a little pause, and then the Professor went on: —

"And now we must settle what we do. We have here much data, and we must proceed to l ay out our campaign. We know from the inquiry of Jonathan that from the castle to Whitby came fifty boxes of earth, all of which were delivered at Carfax; we also know that at least some of these boxes have been removed. It seems to me, that our first step should be to ascertain whether all the rest remain in the house beyond that wall where we look to-day; or whether any more have been removed. If the latter, we must trace –"

Here we were interrupted in a very startling way. Outside the house came the sound of a pistol-shot; the glass of the window was shattered with a bullet, which, ricocheting from the top of the embrasure, struck the far wall of the room. I am afraid I am at heart a coward, for I shrieked out. The men all jumped to their feet; Lord Godalming flew over to the window and threw up the sash. As he did so we heard Mr. Morris's voice without: —

"Sorry! I fear I have alarmed you. I shall come in and tell you about it." A minute later he came in and said: —

"It was an idiotic thing of me to do, and I ask your pardon, Mrs. Harker, most sincerely; I fear I must have frightened you terribly. But the fact is that whilst the Professor was talking there came a big bat and sat on the window-sill. I have got such a horror of the damned brutes from recent events that I cannot stand them, and I went out to have a shot, as I have been doing of late of evenings whenever I have seen one. You used to laugh at me for it then, Art."

"Did you hit it?" asked Dr. Van Helsing.

"I don't know; I fancy not, for it flew away into the wood." Without saying any more he took his seat, and the Professor began to resume his statement: —

"We must trace each of these boxes; and when we are ready, we must either capture or kill this monster in his lair; or we must, so to speak, sterilize the earth, so that no more he can seek safety in it. Thus in the end we may find him in his form of man between the hours of noon and sunset, and so engage with him when he is at his most weak.

"And now for you, Madam Mina, this night is the end until all be well. You are too precious to us to have such risk. When we part to-night, you no more must question. We shall tell you all in good time. We are men, and are able to bear; but you must be our star and our hope, and we shall act all the more free that you are not in the danger, such as we are."

All the men, even Jonathan, seemed relieved; but it did not seem to me good that they should brave danger and, perhaps, lessen their safety – strength being the best safety – through care of me; but their minds were made up, and, though it was a bitter pill for me to swallow, I could say nothing, save to accept their chivalrous care of me.

Mr. Morris resumed the discussion: —

"As there is no time to lose, I vote we have a look at his house right now. Time is everything with him; and swift action on our part may save another victim."

I own that my heart began to fail me when the time for action came so close, but I did not say anything, for I had a greater fear that if I appeared as a drag or a hindrance to their work, they might even leave me out of their counsels altogether. They have now gone off to Carfax, with means to get into the house.

Manlike, they have told me to go to bed and sleep; as if a woman can sleep when those she loves are in danger! I shall lie down and pretend to sleep, lest Jonathan have added anxiety about me when he returns.

Dr. Van Helsing's Memorandum

15 November, afternoon. – I am at least sane. Thank God for that mercy at all events, though the proving it has been dreadful. When I left Madam Mina sleeping within the Holy circle, I took my way to the castle. The blacksmith hammer which I took in the carriage from Veresti was useful; though the doors were all open I broke them off the rusty hinges, lest some ill-intent or ill-chance should close them, so that being entered I might not get out. Jonathan's bitter experience served me here. By memory of his diary I found my way to the old chapel, for I knew that here my work lay. The air was oppressive; it seemed as if there was some sulphurous fume, which at times made me dizzy. Either there was a roaring in my ears or I heard afar off the howl of wolves. Then I bethought me of my dear Madam Mina, and I was in terrible plight. The dilemma had me between his horns. Her, I had not dare to take into this place, but left safe from the Vampire in that Holy circle; and yet event here would be the wolf! I resolve me that my work lay here, and that as to the wolves we must submit, if it were God's Will. At any rate it was only death and freedom beyond. So did I choose for her. Had it but been for myself the choice had been easy; the maw of the wolf were better to rest in than the grave of the Vampire! So I make my choice to go on with my work.

I knew that there were at least three graves to find – graves that are inhabit; so I search, and search, and I find one of them. She lay in her Vampire sleep, so full of life and voluptuous beauty that I shudder as though I have come to do murder. Ah, I doubt not that in old time, when such things were, many a man who set forth to do such a task as mine, found at the last his heart fail him, and then his nerve. So he delay, and delay, and delay, till the mere beauty and the fascination of the wanton Un-Dead have hypnotize him; and he remain on, and on, till sunset come, and the Vampire sleep be over. Then the beautiful eyes of the fair woman open and look love, and the voluptuous mouth present to a kiss – and man is weak. And there remain one more victim in the Vampire fold; one more to swell the grim and grisly ranks of the Un-Dead!...

There is some fascination, surely, when I am moved by the mere presence of such an one, even lying as she lay in a tomb fretted with age and heavy with the dust of centuries though there be that horrid odor such as the lairs of the Count have had. Yes, I was moved – I, Van Helsing, with all my purpose and with my motive for hate – I was moved to a yearning for delay which seemed to paralyze my faculties and to clog my very soul. It may have been that the need of natural sleep, and the strange oppression of the air, were beginning to overcome me. Certain it was that I was lapsing into sleep, the open-eyed sleep of one who yields to a sweet fascination, when there came through the snow-stilled air a long, low wail, so full of woe and pity that it woke me like the sound of a clarion. For it was the voice of my dear Madam Mina that I heard.

Then I braced myself again to my horrid task, and found by wrenching away tomb-tops one other of the sisters, the other dark one. I dared not pause to look on her as I had on her sister, lest once more I should begin to be enthrall; but I go on searching until, presently, I find in a high great tomb as if made to one much beloved that other fair sister which, like Jonathan, I had seen to gather herself out of the atoms of the mist. She was so fair to look on, so radiantly beautiful, so exquisitely voluptuous, that the very instinct of man in me, which calls some of my sex to love and to protect one of hers, made my head whirl with new emotion. But, God be thanked, that soul-wail of my dear Madam Mina had not died out of my ears; and, before the spell could be wrought further upon me, I had nerved myself to my wild work. By this time I had searched all the tombs in the chapel, so far as I could tell; and as there had been only three of these Un-Dead phantoms around us in the night, I took it that there were no more of active Un-Dead existent. There was one great tomb more lordly than all the rest; huge it was, and nobly proportioned. On it was but one word,

DRACULA

This then was the Un-Dead home of the King-Vampire, to whom so many more were due. Its emptiness spoke eloquent to make certain what I knew. Before I began to restore these women to their dead selves through my awful work, I laid in Dracula's tomb some of the Wafer, and so banished him from it, Undead for ever.

Then began my terrible task, and I dreaded it. Had it been but one, it had been easy, comparative. But three! To begin

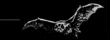

twice more after I had been through a deed of horror; for if it was terrible with the sweet Miss Lucy, what would it not be with these strange ones who had survived through centuries, and who had been strengthened by the passing of the years; who would, if they could, have fought for their foul lives?...

Oh, my friend John, but it was butcher work; had I not been nerved by thoughts of other dead, and of the living over whom hung such a pall of fear, I could not have gone on. I tremble, and tremble even yet, though till all was over, God be thanked, my nerve did stand. Had I not seen the repose in the first face, and the gladness that stole over it just ere the final dissolution came, as realization that the soul had been won, I could not have gone further with my butchery. I could not have endured the horrid screeching as the stake drove home; the lunging of writhing form, and the lips of bloody foam. I should have fled in terror and left my work undone. But it is over! And the poor soul, I can pity them now and weep, as I think of them placid each in her full sleep of death, for a short moment ere fading. For, friend John, hardly had my knife severed the head of each, before the whole body began to melt away and crumble into its native dust, as though the death that should have come centuries agone had at last assert himself and say at once and loud "I am her!"

Before I left the castle I so fixed its entrances that never more can the Count enter there Un-Dead.

When I stepped into the circle where Madam Mina slept, she woke from her sleep, and seeing me, cried out in pain that I had endured too much.

"Come!" she said, "come away form this awful place! Let us go to meet my husband, who is, I know, coming towards us." She was looking thin and pale and weak; but her eyes were pure and glowed with fervor. I was glad to see her paleness and her illness, for my mind was full of the fresh horror of that ruddy Vampire sleep.

And so with trust and hope, and yet full of fear, we go eastward to meet our friends – and him – whom Madam Mina tell me that she know are coming to meet us.

Mina Harker's Journal

6 November. – It was late in the afternoon when the Professor and I took our way towards the east whence I knew Jonathan was coming. We did not go fast, though the way was steeply downhill, for we had to take heavy rugs and wraps with us; we dared not face the possibility of being left without warmth in the cold and the snow. We had to take some of our provisions too, for we were in a perfect desolation, and, so far as we could see through the snowfall, there was not even the sign of a habitation. When we had gone about a mile, I was tired with the heavy walking and sat down to rest. Then we looked back and saw where the clear line of Dracula's castle cut the sky; for we were so deep under the hill whereon it was set that the angle of perspective of the Carpathian Mountains was far below it. We saw it in all its grandeur, perched a thousand feet on the summit of a sheer precipice, and with seemingly a great gap between it and the steep of the adjacent mountain on any side. There was something wild and uncanny about the place. We could hear the distant howling of wolves. They were far off, but the sound, even though coming muffled through the deadening snowfall, was full of terror. I knew from the way Dr. Van Helsing was searching about that he was trying to seek some strategic point, where we would be less exposed in case of attack. The rough roadway still led downwards; we could trace it though the drifted snow.

In a little while the Professor signaled to me, so I got up and joined him. He had found a wonderful spot, a sort of natural hollow in a rock, with an entrance like a doorway between the two boulders. He took me by the hand and drew me in: "See!" he said, "here you will be in a shelter; and if the wolves do come I can meet them one by one." He brought in our furs, and made a snug nest for me, and got out some provisions and forced them upon me. But I could not eat; to even try to do so was repulsive to me, and, much as I would have liked to please him, I could not bring myself to the attempt. He looked very sad, but did not reproach me. Taking his field-glasses from the case, he stood on the top of the rock, and began to search the horizon. Suddenly he called out: —

"Look Madam Mina, look! Look!" I sprang up and stood beside him on the rock; he handed me his glasses and pointed. The snow was now falling more heavily, and swirled about fiercely, for a high wind was beginning to blow. However, there were times when there were pauses between the snow flurries, and I could see a long way round. From the height where we were it was possible to see a great distance; and lying like a black ribbon in kinks and curls as it wound its way. Straight in front of us and not far off – in fact so near that I wondered we had not noticed before – came a group of mounted men hurrying along. In the midst of them was a dog's tail wagging, with each stern inequality of the road. Outlined against the snow as they wee, I could see from the men's clothes that they were peasants of gypsies of some kind.

On the cart was a great square chest. My heart leaped as I saw it, for I felt that the end was coming. The evening was now drawing close, and well I knew that at sunset the Thing, which was till then imprisoned there, would take new freedom and could in any of many forms elude all pursuit. In fear I turned to the Professor; to my consternation, however, he was not there. An instant later, I saw him below me. Round the rock he had drawn a circle, such as we had found shelter in last night. When he had completed it he stood beside me again, saying: —

"At least you shall be safe here from him! He took the glasses from me, and at the next lull of the snow swept the whole space below us. "See," he said, "they come quickly; they are flogging the horses, and galloping as hard as they can." He paused and went on in a hollow voice: —

"They are racing for the sunset. We may be too late. God's will be done!" Down came another blinding rush of driving snow, and the whole landscape was blotted out. It soon passed, however, and once more his glasses were fixed on the plan. Then came a sudden cry: —

"Look! Look! Look! See, two horsemen follow fast, coming up from the south. It must be Quincey and John. Take the glass. Look, before the snow blots it all out!" I took it and looked. The two men might be Dr. Seward and Mr. Morris. I knew at all events that neither of them was Jonathan. At the same time I knew that Jonathan was not far off; looking around I saw on the north side of the coming party two other men, riding at break-neck speed. One of them I knew was Jonathan, and the other I took, of course, to be Lord Godalming. They, too, were pursuing the party with the cart. When I told the Professor he shouted in glee like a schoolboy, and after looking intently till snowfall made sight impossible, he laid his

Winchester rifle ready for use against the boulder at the opening of our shelter. "They are all converging," he said. "When the time comes we shall have the gypsies on all sides." I got out my revolver ready to hand, for whilst we were speaking the howling of wolves came louder and closer. When the snowstorm abated a moment we looked again. It was strange to see the snow falling in such heavy flakes close to us, and beyond, the sun shining more and more brightly as it sank down towards the far mountain tops. Sweeping the glass all around us I could see here and there dots moving singly in twos and threes and larger numbers – the wolves were gathering for they prey.

Every instant seemed an age whilst we waited. The wind came now in fierce bursts, and the snow was driven with fury as it swept upon us in circling eddies. At times we could not see an arm's length before us; but at others as the hollow-sounding wind swept by us, it seemed to clear the air-space around us so that we could see afar off. We had of late been so accustomed to watch for sunrise and sunset that we knew with fair accuracy when it would be; and we knew that before long the sun would set.

It was hard to believe that by our watches it was less than an hour that we waited in that rocky shelter before the various bodies began to converge close upon us. The wind came now with fiercer and more bitter sweeps, and more steadily from the north. It seemingly had driven the snow-clouds from us, for, with only occasional bursts, the snow fell. We could distinguish clearly the individuals of each party, the pursued and the pursuers. Strangely enough those pursued did not seem to realize, or at least to care, that they were pursued; they seemed, however, to hasten with redoubled speed as the sun dropped lower and lower on the mountain tops.

Closer and closer they drew. The Professor and I crouched down behind our rock, and held our weapons ready; I could see that he was determined that they should not pass. One and all were quite unaware of our presence.

All at once two voices shouted out to "Halt!" One was my Jonathan's, raised in a high key of passion; the other, Mr. Morris's strong resolute tone of quiet command. The gypsies may not have known the language, but there was no mistaking the tone, in whatever tongue the words were spoken. Instinctively they reined in, and at the instant Lord Godalming and Jonathan dashed up at one side and Dr. Seward and Mr. Morris on the other. The leader of the gypsies, a splendid-looking fellow, who sat his horse like a centaur, waved some word to proceed. They lashed the horses, which sprang forward; but the four men raised the Winchester rifles, and in an unmistakable way commanded them to stop. At the same moment Dr. Van Helsing and I rose behind the rock and pointed our weapons at them. Seeing that they were surrounded, the men tightened their reins and drew up. The leader turned to them and gave a word, at which every man of the gypsy party drew what weapon he carried, knife or pistol, and held himself in readiness to attack. Issue was joined in an instant.

The leader, with a quick movement of his rein, threw his horse out in front, and pointing first to the sun – now close down on the hill-tops – and then to the castle, said something which I did not understand. For answer all four men of our party threw themselves from their horses and dashed towards the cart. I should have felt terrible fear at seeing Jonathan in such danger, but that the ardor of battle must have been upon me as well as the rest of them; I felt no fear, but only a wild, surging desire to do something. Seeing a quick movement of our parties, the leader of the gypsies gave a command; his men instantly formed round the cart in a sort of undisciplined endeavor, each one shouldering and pushing the other in his eagerness to carry out the order.

In the midst of this I could see that Jonathan on one side of the ring of men, and Quincey on the other, were forcing a way to the cart; it was evident that they were bent on finishing their task before the sun should set. Nothing seemed to stop or even to hinder them. Neither the leveled weapons or the flashing knives of the gypsies in front, or the howling of the wolves behind, appeared to even attract their attention. Jonathan's impetuosity, and the manifest singleness of his purpose, seemed to overawe those in front of him; instinctively they cowered aside and let him pass. In an instant he had jumped upon the cart, and, with a strength which seemed incredible, raised the great box, and flung it over the wheel to the ground. In the meantime, Mr. Morris had had to use force to pass through his side of the ring of Szgany. All the time I had been breathlessly watching Jonathan I had, with the tail of my eye, seen him pressing desperately forward, and had seen the knives of the gypsies flash as he won a way through them, and they cut at him. He parried with his great bowie knife, and at first I thought that he too had come through in safety, but as he sprang beside Jonathan, who had by now jumped from the cart, I could see that with his left hand he was clutching at his side, and that the blood was spurting through his fingers.

He did not delay notwithstanding this, for as Jonathan, with desperate energy, attacked one end of the chest, attempting to prise off the lid with his great Kukri knife, he attacked the other frantically with his bowie. Under the efforts of both men the lid began to yield; the nails drew with a quick screeching sound, and the top of the box was thrown back.

By this time the gypsies, seeing themselves covered by the Winchesters, and at the mercy of Lord Godalming and Dr. Seward, had given in and made no further resistance. The sun was almost down on the mountain tops, and the shadows of the whole group fell long upon the snow. I saw the Count lying within the box upon the earth, some of which the rude falling from the cart had scattered over him. He was deathly pale, just like a waxen image, and the red eyes glared with the horrible vindictive look which I knew too well.

As I looked, the eyes saw the sinking sun, and the look of hate in them turned to triumph.

But, on the instant, came the sweep and flash of Jonathan's great knife. I shrieked as I saw it shear through the throat; whilst at the same moment Mr. Morris' bowie knife plunged in the heart.

It was like a miracle; but before our very eyes, and almost in the drawing of a breath, the whole body crumbled into dust and passed from our sight.

I shall be glad as long as I live that even in that moment of final dissolution there was in the face a look of peace, such as I never could have imagined might have rested there.

The Castle of Dracula now stood out against the red sky, and every stone of its broken battlements was articulated against the light of the setting sun.

They gypsies, taking us as in some way the cause of the extraordinary disappearance of the dead man, turned, without a word, and rode away as if for their lives. Those who were unmounted jumped upon the leiter-waggon and shouted to the horsemen not to desert them. The wolves, which had withdrawn to a safe distance, followed in their wake, leaving us alone.

Mr. Morris, who had sunk to the ground, leaned on his elbow, holding his hand pressed to his side; the blood still gushed through his fingers. I flew to him, for the Holy circle did not now keep me back; so did the two doctors. Jonathan knelt behind him and the wounded man laid back his head on his shoulder. With a sigh he took, with a feeble effort, my hand in that of his own which was unstained.

He must have seen the anguish of my heart in my face, for he smiled at me and said: —

"I am only too happy to have been of any service! Oh, God!" he cried suddenly, struggling up to a sitting posture and pointing to me, "it was worth this to die! Look! Look!"

The sun was now right down upon the mountain top, and the red gleams fell upon my face, so that it was bathed in rosy light. With one impulse the men sank on their knees, and a deep earnest "Amen" broke from all as their eyes followed the pointing of his finger as the dying man spoke: —

"Now God be thanked that all has not been in vain! See! The snow is not more stainless than her forehead! The curse has passed away!"

And, to our bitter grief, with a smile and silence, he died, a gallant gentleman. ...

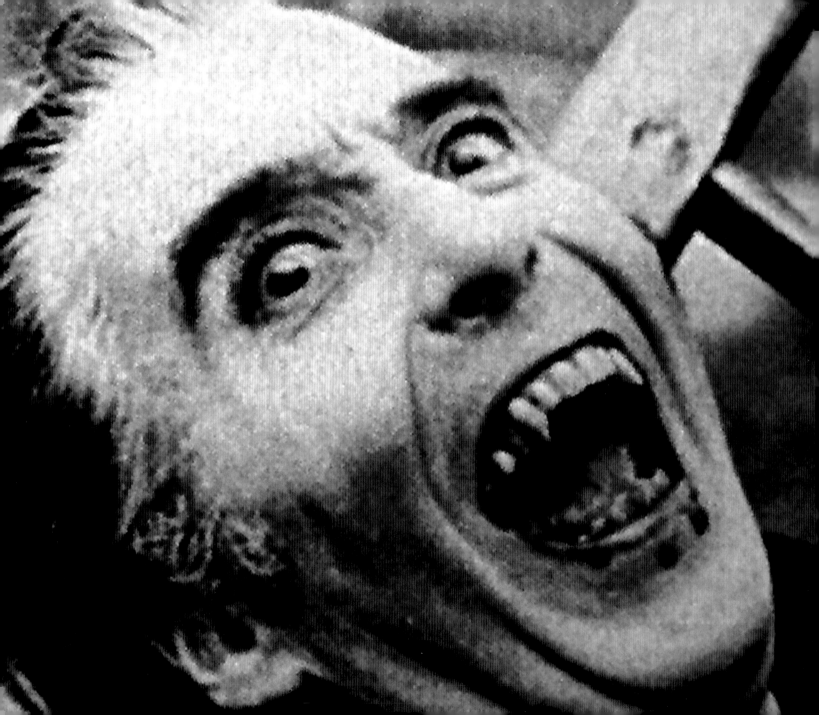